SAUSAGE & MASH

FIONA BECKETT

PHOTOGRAPHY BY GEORGIA GLYNN-SMITH

TO MOPSY,
WHO LOVED A GOOD SAUSAGE.

SAUSAGE & MASH

FIONA BECKETT

PHOTOGRAPHY BY GEORGIA GLYNN-SMITH

Absolute Press

First published in Great Britain in 2004 by
Absolute Press
Scarborough House
29 James Street West
Bath BA1 2BT
Phone 44 (0) 1225 316013
Fax 44 (0) 1225 445836
E-mail info@absolutepress.co.uk
Website www.absolutepress.co.uk

Publisher Jon Croft
Commissioning Editor Meg Avent
Art Direction Matt Inwood
Photography Georgia Glynn-Smith
Home Economist David Morgan
Stylist Liz Belton

A catalogue record of this book is available from the
British Library

ISBN 1 904573 18 5

Printed and bound by Printer Trento, Italy

CONTENTS

07 INTRODUCTION
21 POTATOES, ROOTS & GREENS
65 PIZZA, PASTA & PIES
89 RICE, BEANS & GRAINS
109 FEASTS
141 OTHER SAUSAGE-RELATED MATTERS
155 INDEX
159 ACKNOWLEDGMENTS/ CONVERSION TABLE

08   THE ULTIMATE COMFORT FOOD
09   WHAT MAKES A GREAT SAUSAGE?
12   THE WORLD'S BEST SAUSAGES
16   HOW TO COOK A GOOD SAUSAGE

INTRODUCTION

THE ULTIMATE COMFORT FOOD

There isn't anyone I've told about this book
who hasn't looked dreamily into the middle distance and said
I *love* sausage and mash. It has to be the ultimate comfort food
– the sausages plump and sticky from long, slow cooking, the
mash light and buttery, the onion gravy rich, dark and savoury.
Every mouthful (which should include a little of each) pure,
unadulterated bliss. But unless you've been living in the depths
of the Amazonian rainforests (or what remains of them) for the
last five years, you will have observed that sausages have
changed. For the better, on the whole. Now you can buy
authentic French, Italian or Spanish sausages. You can buy
inauthentic but delicious Thai or Indian-spiced sausages.
You can buy beef, lamb or venison sausages. Gluten-free
sausages, low-fat or organic sausages. Big sausages.
Small sausages. You can buy almost any sausage under
the sun. Which means you can do a lot more with them
than you could with just a plain old porker.

In this book I've tried to combine the best of the old with the
best of the new. Good old fashioned favourites like Sausage
Onion and Apple Pie, Toad in the Hole and Hot Dogs.
Some continental classics such as Italian Sausage, Tomato
and Basil Risotto, Cassoulet and Sausages with Puy Lentils.
Original ideas such as Thai Sausages with Leek and
Lemongrass Rice and Chinese-style Sausages with Stir-fried
Greens. Sausages turned into meatballs, pasta sauces and
pies. There are elegant sausage meals for two, and family
meals for four or more. There are ideas for sausage-based
breakfasts, barbecues, picnics and parties. For cold days
and hot days and Christmas Day. In short, there are recipes
for every sausage-related occasion.

The only thing you won't find in this book is information
about dry-cured sausages like salamis (I had to stop somewhere)
or much about sausages I don't like (so no andouillette or
drisheen). This is a book for sausage-lovers rather than sausage
connoisseurs or those who want to make sausages of their
own. It's not a sausage guide either, though you will find out
plenty about the sausages I rate. It's a personal take on the
sausage world.

Finally a note on quantities. It's been particularly difficult with
this book as I know that most sausage lovers' capacity to eat
sausages goes way – and sometimes disastrously – beyond
other foods and that you may deliberately want to create
leftovers. But I've assumed two can polish off a 400g pack
of sausages – three at a pinch, depending how meaty they
are and what you serve with them. If you disagree then it's
simply a question of buying a couple more....

Fiona Beckett, August 2004

WHAT MAKES A GREAT SAUSAGE?

When I thought about what makes a great sausage, I was tempted to say the kind of sausages we all had as children, but that's not strictly true. As someone who was brought up on Wall's skinless – a smooth, pink pasty sausage – I can't say I yearn for them now. But certainly tradition and nostalgia have a part to play. For instance, most British have a fondness for a simple chipolata that I doubt is replicated anywhere else in the world.

A good sausage should of course start with good meat. Not that it always does. If you pay the 49p for 570g of economy sausages that one leading supermarket currently charges you're not going to get a lot for it. The meat content of a pork sausage in the UK only has to be 42% of which 30% can be fat and 25% 'connective tissue'. That of a beef or lamb sausage can be even less – a mere 30%. As food writer Tessa Boase put it in a shocking exposé she wrote for the *Daily Mail* as a result of an undercover stint in a sausage factory:

'When you choose a pack of pink, textureless, mass-produced sausages you buy into a miserable chain of degradation: from the antibiotic-pumped pig crammed into a factory farm, to the impoverished meat, the chemical additives, indifferent hygiene and cheap labour. It is a chain which, ultimately, holds the consumer in cynical contempt.'

A good butcher will use, by contrast, whole pieces of lean meat with a significant proportion of sweet-tasting back fat (about one third). 'The secret of a great sausage is fat' says Paul Hughes, who makes sausages for London-based butcher The Ginger Pig (*see* p152). 'If a sausage is too lean it won't hold together. People obviously assume that fat makes a sausage fatty. But there are types of fat such as back fat that don't taste fatty and that is what we use.' The lean component is chunks of leg, shoulder and belly, all from pigs that are raised on their own farm in North Yorkshire and reared as naturally as possible. Most butchers mince their meat but there is a school of thought that nothing beats hand-chopped meat in a sausage.

Unlike most continental sausages the traditional British sausage is made with a high proportion of dried rusk. That's not necessarily a bad thing as it creates the smooth-textured British sausage we're used to and may at times (like breakfast) prefer. It also keeps the price down. But it does mean the sausage will contain a significant proportion of water to reconstitute it. In theory, the water content shouldn't exceed the weight of the rusk, though some ingredients lists on sausage packs show that it's the second largest ingredient. Ice is also used in many cheaper sausages to keep the temperature of the meat down during mixing which is why so many sausages seem wet. A decent sausage, however, should contain at least 65% of meat, a really good one 80-90%.

Seasoning was traditionally simple – salt, pepper (usually white) and mace lie at the heart of most British sausages, with certain regions using dried herbs such as sage (*see* p12).
Now, with the explosion of different flavours, most butchers rely on bought-in packs of seasoning from the large flavouring companies. This is understandable – they are, at the end of the day, butchers rather than chefs and many lack the skill to create their own recipes. Pre-mixes also give a product a longer shelf life but they may mean your sausage will contain many ingredients you wouldn't particularly want to be there if you made them yourself. Including too much salt.

Some of these ingredients owe more to E-numbers than anything that resembles the storecupboard of flavourings available to the keen cook. As Hugh Fearnley-Whittingstall puts it his *River Cottage Meat Book,*

'Cheap sausages may sometimes seem moreish not because of any real quality they possess but because of the combination of the comfort of familiarity and the deceptive, almost hallucinatory effect on the taste buds of artificial flavours and preservatives such as monosodium glutamate, dextrose and E numbers. As with bad Chinese food and cheese and onion crisps there is a shallow pharmaceutical gratification of

the taste buds but little, if any, lasting pleasure or satisfaction.' Does that mean a good sausage shouldn't be a flavoured sausage? I wouldn't go as far as that. But in the quest for novelty there are some increasingly bizarre combinations being developed that don't have any integrity. It creates another good argument (the first obviously being the quality of the meat) for sticking to premium lines at supermarkets and finding a butcher who uses their own, preferably fresh, seasonings. And maybe getting your buzz from the ingredients you put with your sausages rather than in them so that you actually get to taste the meat.

Other ingredients that go into most mass produced sausages are colour (have you ever seen pork as pink as the pork you get in cheap sausages?) and preservative. Again, there's a logic to that, but you do have to wonder about the quantities they're using when you can buy a pack of sausages that doesn't need to be eaten until 11 days later. And will presumably have taken 2-3 days to reach the shelf.

The final element in a sausage is the casing. This will either be natural – sheeps' intestines for chipolatas and thin sausages such as Merguez, pigs' intestines for bigger sausages – or synthetic. Most cheap sausages are made with synthetic casings made from collagen or beef protein which may well come from outside the UK – another potential cause for unease.

A good sausage is also a well made sausage – just watch the skills employed as a good butcher deftly twists and bunches a long coil of sausage into the traditional links. Technically, a good sausage should be evenly filled without any bumps or air pockets – by no means as easy as it seems. The butcher has to control the flow of meat from the mixer into the slithery skins with a knee-operated pedal, stopping it pumping out too fast 'and seeing 140 feet of sausage suddenly coiling off into the distance', as Paul Hughes of the Ginger Pig puts it. It looks like one of those impossible tasks they set contestants on game shows and, lacking that kind of nimble dexterity, is one of the reasons I don't make my own sausages.

It's also worth finding out when your sausages have been made – and buying them a day later. Sausages need 24 hours to dry out otherwise they can burst when you fry them (*see* p16).

If you really care about the quality of your sausages there is nothing to beat sourcing them from a reliable supplier you would trust to supply the rest of your meat. Because sausages are so detached from the animal, I fear that we sometimes make them a special case, suspending our moral standards about knowing where our meat comes from. But we shouldn't.

Many producers are now rearing so-called rare (though increasingly common) breeds such as Gloucester Old Spot, Tamworth, Berkshire and Middle White, pigs that take longer to develop but whose meat is much more flavourful and are likely to have been reared to humane standards.

Again, my model sausage maker, The Ginger Pig, sells sausages that come from their own herd of beguilingly red-coated Tamworth pigs. Owners Tim and Anne Wilson are farmers who also grow their own feed which is antibiotic and GM-free. And although they are not registered as organic they try as hard as they can to make sure that the end product is the very best that it can be and that the animals themselves are looked after properly.

It makes a more expensive sausage, certainly, but even the most expensive sausage is good value compared to premium cuts of meat such as steaks, chops or roasts and being meatier you eat less of them. If you don't have a good local butcher, then these days you can easily buy them online or by mail order (*see* p152). There really is no excuse....

THE WORLD'S BEST SAUSAGES

Every sausage-producing country has its own traditions and preferences which vary not only from region to region but butcher to butcher. I couldn't possibly do justice to them all but here are the types of fresh sausage you're most likely to come across.

GREAT BRITAIN & IRELAND

As already explained, we Brits like a breadier sausage than our continental counterparts. Traditionally these would have been fairly plain, seasoned with salt, white pepper, mace and maybe some sage. The Cambridge sausage is a typical and popular example, though it may not always be labelled as such. A slight variation in ingredients – in this case the inclusion of sage and cayenne pepper – is enough to give it an identity of its own. Oxford sausages, by contrast, were made with a mixture of pork, veal and suet, flavoured with herbs and lemon rind and were always skinless, while Lincolnshire sausages have always been distinguished by their heavy use of sage. There are also sausages, such as the Newmarket, which owe their status to the energy and enterprise of local butchers – in this specific instance, Musk's, which was founded in 1884.

Other sausages would have been based on a specific breed of pig and survived even when the breed itself became extinct. The classic example is the Cumberland, a coarsely ground sausage with a high meat content, traditionally sold in a coil, which remains, in my view, one of the great British bangers.

Scots have always preferred a beef sausage, the most distinctive type being the square, skinless Lorne sausage sold in slices and named, according to Laura Mason and Catherine Brown's *Traditional Foods of Britain*, after comedian Tommy Lorne. 'Its square, flat shape was a convenient fit for a morning roll along with a fried egg' they write. (Although I've heard it described as a Lorne sausage elsewhere, Mason and Brown claim it's only known as Lorne sausage in Glasgow. Elsewhere in Scotland it is simply known as square or sliced sausage.) A modern, upmarket equivalent is the Aberdeen Angus sausage which has become increasingly widely available on supermarket shelves.

There is also a strong tradition all over the British Isles and Ireland of sausages made from offal, the most famous being haggis and black pudding. Haggis, is made (and you may rather not know this) from sheeps innards, mixed with oatmeal, suet and onions and stuffed in a sheep's stomach – a less gamey, more appetising version of the French andouillette. Black pudding is a robustly spiced blood sausage made with oats or barley, onions and herbs (traditionally marjoram, thyme, pennyroyal and mint), often designed to be sliced rather than eaten whole. Its heartland is in Lancashire, especially round the town of Bury where long-established family firms still sell off stalls in the market. White or 'mealy' puddings which are based on oatmeal and pork fat may not include any lean meat at all, or very little. That said, they're suprisingly tasty – my favourite being the Irish Clonakilty white pudding.

FRANCE

The French sausage world is confusingly divided into the similar sounding saucisse and saucisson, both of which, according to the *Oxford Companion to Food,* have fresh and dried varieties. Saucisse traditionally refers to smaller sausages and saucisson to larger ones. In practice the former generally means a fresh sausage which is the only type we shall concern ourselves with.

Typically, the saucisse will be an all-meat affair, coarsely cut with quite a high percentage of fat – good for cooking on the grill. The one we come across most often is the meaty Toulouse, although British supermarkets and butchers tend to add ingredients that are not in the original, which is simply based on chopped meat, salt, white pepper, sugar and saltpetre. Garlic and herbs are Anglo-Saxon additions.

The other increasingly popular French import is Merguez, a spicy Algerian lamb sausage seasoned with hot pepper. It is generally made in lamb's casings, so is chipolata-sized and goes exceptionally well with couscous.

The French also have their own black and white pudding, boudin noir and boudin blanc, which tend to be smoother and more delicately flavoured than their English counterparts. Boudins blancs are in fact quite a gourmet treat and may be made, according to Antony and Araminta Hippisley Coxe's *Book of Sausages*, with 'pork and chicken, veal, rabbit, hare, cream, onions, eggs and breadcrumbs or ground rice.' They are poached then fried just before serving. Like the locals we buy them flavoured with truffles to go with our Christmas turkey.

The other famous French sausage is andouillette, which like haggis is made from intestines, though pigs' and calves' rather than sheep's. It is, I think it is safe to say, an acquired taste. Not one acquired by me.

ITALY

Like French sausages, fresh Italian sausages or salsiccie tend to be made exclusively of meat, usually pork. The seasoning can vary quite intriguingly though, often from village to village. Garlic and fennel seeds are popular flavourings in the centre of Italy, while in the south and Sicily sausages are often flavoured with hot peppers. A distinctive style – commonly sold in Italian delis – is the Luganega or Luganeghe which is sold in a coil like a Cumberland sausage and tastes particularly good grilled or oven-roasted. Being meaty and well flavoured, Italian sausages make a good basis for a pasta sauce or risotto (*see* pp64-70 and p90).

Other types you may come across include Cotechino, a large boiling sausage from the Emilia Romagna region and zampone which is stuffed in a pig's trotter, both of which are slightly gelatinous. Most of the ones that arrive here simply have to be re-heated. Traditionally they're served with lentils.

SPAIN AND PORTUGAL

Hot pepper or pimenton is the characteristic seasoning of Spanish and Portuguese chorizo or chourico sausages, both fresh and dried. There are over 50 types in Spain alone, which vary in degrees of hotness. If you're cooking them it's important to buy the fresh version (*see* p153), which is obviously softer than the dried one, though still harder and drier than a fresh French or Italian sausage. Because they hold their shape well they're good for barbecuing and can be used in soups and stews, especially with beans. Even quite a small amount will give a dish an intense flavour. You'll also find them featured in Latin American recipes.

Morcilla is Spain's famous black pudding, strongly spiced and particularly delicious. According to importers Brindisa (*see* p153) it may contain a wide variety of ingredients, depending on which area of Spain it comes from; 'these can include potatoes or squash, almonds, nuts, cinnamon, garlic, onions or rice, or a combination of these ingredients'. The Portuguese equivalent is morcelas.

GERMANY & USA

Germany must be the world's most serious sausage-producing nation with over 1000 different varieties, many of which don't make their way here. Most, like the famous frankfurter, which is made of pork and beef flavoured with salt, onion, mace, pepper, saltpetre and sugar, are smoked and scalded in boiling water, then simply have to be re-heated – or stuffed into hot dogs. Bratwurst – or brats as they're called in the states, where they have been popularised by German immigrants – are a light grilling sausage, unsmoked and made from pork or pork and veal. The most historic ones come from the towns of Nuremberg and Thuringen, which has recently celebrated its 600th year of sausage making. Apparently, the southern German equivalent is called weisswurst.

OTHER NOTABLE SAUSAGES

After the Germans, the Poles are the world's leading sausage producers, making a huge range of smoked sausages such as kabanos and kielbasa (also popular in the USA). These tend to be harder than their German equivalents, but are served in a similar way, lentils also being a favoured accompaniment.

Various spicy sausages are made round the eastern Mediterranean in Greece, Cyprus and Turkey and served as a meze. The best known – which you often come across in Greek or Cypriot restaurants – is loukanika, a particularly tasty sausage made from pork, marinated in red wine and flavoured with coriander and herbs. In Turkey they have bastourma which is made with lamb and flavoured with paprika.

Another excellent spicy sausage is the South African boerewors, traditionally a pork and beef sausage which is particularly good for barbecues. Many butchers now make a version during the summer.

The Chinese also have a distinctive style of sausage which you can find in Chinese supermarkets, the best known of which is lap cheung. It's quite dry, so needs to be steamed or sliced thinly and stir-fried. (The Chinese steam it over rice.) It can be quite spicy.

HOW TO COOK A GOOD SAUSAGE

Everyone has their own idea of how to cook a perfect sausage, often stubbornly adhered to, despite suggestions that another method might be more successful or convenient. They're driven not only by the desire for culinary perfection but also time, health consciousness and the dislike of smell and spattering fat. All deep-rooted prejudices, so I'm not going to be dictatorial about this, but simply explore the pros and cons of each technique.

GRILLING

Grilling is the most popular method of cooking sausages, according to a recent report from the Meat and Livestock Commission, with 44% of all respondents choosing to pop their sausages under the grill. This presumably (although the report doesn't say so) is the result of a belief that this makes them less fatty, though another report by the Food Standards Agency suggests this isn't the case.

The method does have noted champions, such as Antony and Araminta Hippisley Coxe, authors of the *Book of Sausages,* and does produce a drier sausage which some obviously prefer (though not me). It's also relatively quick, about 15-20 minutes under a moderate grill, but not a hot one, otherwise you may get a sausage that is burnt on the outside and raw inside, or, equally critical, a flare-up and a kitchen full of smoke. For the same reason you shouldn't put the sausages too near the grill.

Incidentally, in your quest for a leaner sausage you shouldn't prick them, a notion that dates from the post-war period when sausages were very poor quality and there was plenty of fat to leach out. As *Guardian* food writer and sausage aficionado Matthew Fort succinctly put it in his *Sausage Directory*, published in 1992, 'If you do, you will only allow a good deal of the natural juices to flow out during cooking, making the inside drier and lessening the flavour.'

There is also, of course, grilling in the sense of barbecuing, but that's another subject on which you should consult pp126-128.

FRYING

This is the technique preferred by the two oracles I respect in all matters sausage-related, Matthew Fort and Nigel Slater. And by me. As Nigel puts it in his *Real Food* 'the scrumptious goo that is built up on the outside is the whole point of eating a sausage and cannot be properly achieved by grilling.' Unfortunately, this scrumptious goo takes time, 40-50 minutes, advises Fort,: a rather more modest 25 minutes, in Nigel's case. I'm with Nigel on this. Sausages are, when it comes down to it, a convenience food and 40 minutes is a long time to hover over a pan, turning your sausages to make sure they brown evenly. On the other hand a good sausage can't be rushed. You don't want to turn the heat up or you won't get the goo and they may split and splatter fat all over your cooker.

Either way, you should heat your pan over a moderate heat first before adding the oil (just one tablespoon) and running it around the pan. Then add the sausages, give them a shake so they're lightly coated with oil, turn the heat down and leave them, turning them every 6-7 minutes or so. If you're concerned about your weight (in which case I'm not sure you should be eating sausages anyway) you can spoon off some of the fat that accumulates as you go. The sausages shouldn't split, so long as they're not too fresh.

There is a halfway house which involves less frying, which is to brown your sausage using a little butter as well as the initial oil and then finishing off in a moderate oven (see below). Also a useful method when you want to colour sausages before putting them in a casserole.

BAKING

Baking – the third most popular method of cooking sausages – arouses strong passions. Advocates argue it's convenient, clean, and enables you to cook large numbers of sausages at one fell swoop. Detractors, including Fort, reckons it makes sausages 'as dried and wrinkled as octogenarians in the Florida sun'.

In his 'The Perfect...', based on his columns in the Guardian, Richard Ehrlich argues that a hot oven (at least 200 C/400 F/ Gas 6) is the best way to cook a sausage. He recommends pre-heating a roasting tin with a little oil in it for 5-10 minutes, then putting the sausages in the tin, cooking them for a further 5 minutes, turning them, then continuing to cook them till they're done 'about 10-20 minutes, depending on their girth and the oven's heat.'

The advantage, which accounts for the growing popularity of this technique, is that you're not constantly having to turn the sausages (though Ehrlich acknowledges that extra turns will help them cook more evenly) and that all the spattering fat is contained in the oven. But, by the time you've pre-heated the oven (also quite an expense if you're cooking for one or two) it can take longer than frying or grilling.

Undoubtedly, the baking method is better suited to a sausage with a high meat (and fat) content than an inexpensive high rusk British sausage. You can get round the dryness problem by putting some liquid (wine, stock or cider) in the tin which also helps form a low maintenance gravy (see p34). Alternatively, you can smother the sausages half way through with some kind of sauce (tomato or barbecue) which will provide a gooey and not unappetising coating. (Turn the oven down to 190 C/375 F/Gas 5 if you're cooking them this way.) Accompanying vegetables such as onions, peppers and, of course, potatoes also help, which then turns the dish into a sausage bake (see p48-50).

POACHING

Poaching is the preferred method for cooking Germanic and other Eastern European-style sausages such as frankfurters. Although these are often described as boiled sausages, the water should barely simmer, so it's more akin to poaching.

The method works particularly well with a smoked or semi-dried sausage which has lost some moisture (such as Chinese sausages) but is not at all suitable for soft, wet British sausages. It can also be used for any reasonably firm sausage with a high meat content. Timings will depend on how fat your sausages are to start with. I'd allow 5-6 minutes for a thin frankfurter, 15-20 minutes for a fatter, meatier sausage and 25-30 minutes for a large coil.

The only downside to this technique is the lack of colour in the finished article, but you can remedy this by browning it quickly in a pan with a little butter, or, even better, on a lightly oiled ridged grill or barbecue which will give you fetching chargrilled lines on your sausage. You can also par-boil, or rather, par-poach, sausages you intend to cook on the barbecue (for about half the times given above).

N.B. Whatever way you eventually choose to cook them, though, sausages must always be well done. An underdone sausage is not only a health hazard, it tastes thoroughly nasty too.

22 MASH
24 FLAVOURING MASH
26 MASH WITH ADDITIONS
30 VEGETABLE PURÉES
34 GRAVY
42 SAUSAGE & CHIPS (& OTHER POTATO...)
58 GREENS

POTATOES, ROOTS & GREENS

THE SECRET OF PERFECT MASH

A lot of nonsense is talked about how difficult it is to make really good mash; it isn't difficult, but there are some very useful tips which will help you achieve mash that is both delectably smooth and lump-free.

First of all, the type of potato. There are two schools of thought about this, with some cookery writers and chefs insisting they should be floury and others that they should be waxy. Frankly, it depends what type of mash you want to make. If you want essentially English, fluffy mash use floury ones (I'd suggest King Edward or Kerr's Pink). If you want a French style 'purée' (see Luxury Mash, page 25) use slightly waxy ones like Desirée or Wilja.

Either type will perform better when they're first in season in the autumn. Potatoes that have been in cold storage for 7 or 8 months aren't great for mash – nor are ones that have been lying around in your vegetable rack. In the summer I prefer to use new potatoes to make crushed potatoes, leaving the skins on. (Normally I peel them.)

The main objective is to cook them without them getting too waterlogged. Some steam them but I think that's too much like hard work. You do need to cut them into even-sized pieces though and bring them to the boil in cold water. Once they're boiling turn down the heat to a simmer. Boiling them too fast will make them disintegrate. And when they've cooked, return them to the pan over a very low heat to dry out any excess moisture that will make your spuds soggy.

Mashing should, in my view, be done by hand. Some people use Kenwood-type mixers but that simply creates extra washing up and can make your mash gluey (as can food processors which should never be used for potatoes). Use a fork, potato masher or ricer for the initial mashing, then, after adding extra liquid (usually milk) and butter or oil, use a wooden spoon to whip up the volume, lighten the texture and enrich the flavour of your mash. How much of each liquid you need depends on the gravy situation. If you're serving lashings of

onion gravy I'd go for a drier, plainer mash. If you're serving it with sausages without gravy or with a wine-based 'jus', it'll take a richer, sloppier mash made with whole milk or even cream. Either way the liquid should be hot and the butter at room temperature or melted before you add it.

Finally, how much to make? Well, you know your nearest and dearest better than I do, but a useful rule of thumb is to allow one large potato per person (about 225g) and a slightly smaller one each (about 200g) if you're making a really rich mash. Obviously some people will eat more than this, but then slimmers and carb-avoiders will eat less. Or you hope they will, anyway....

GOOD, EVERYDAY MASH

The whole point about everyday mash is that it should include ingredients you normally have in your home. So, if you use spreadable butter, use that (but not a butter-type spread) and feel free to substitute the whole milk with semi-skimmed milk (adding a dollop or two of crème fraîche for extra richness, if you have some).

900g King Edward or other good boiling
    potatoes
40g of butter at room temperature
50-75ml warm whole (i.e. not skimmed
    or semi-skimmed) milk
Sea salt and freshly ground black pepper

SERVES 4

Peel the potatoes and halve or quarter them so you have even-sized pieces. Put them in a saucepan, cover them with cold water and bring them to the boil (about 5 minutes). Skim off any froth, season them with salt, then cook them for 20-25 minutes until you can put the tip of a knife into them without any resistance.

Drain the potatoes thoroughly in a colander, then return them to the pan and place it over the heat for a few seconds to dry up any excess moisture.

Take the pan off the heat, chop the potatoes up roughly with a knife then mash them with a potato masher or a fork until they are smooth and lump free. (Or, for a finer texture, push them through a ricer.) Beat in the butter and enough warm milk to make a soft but not sloppy consistency (unless, like the French, you like your mash sloppy). Season with salt and freshly ground black pepper.

Once made, your mash will keep happily for 20 minutes in a covered pan.

FLAVOURING YOUR MASH (OR, RATHER, NOT FLAVOURING IT)

I'm conservative about flavoured mash. Mustard, for example, is much better on the side of plate where you can take exactly as much as you want. Cheddar makes mash gluey. Pesto should be reserved for pasta.

These are all inventions of restaurants to make mash sound more interesting so they can charge more for it. They simply disguise the flavour of the potatoes and if you've got gravy you don't need them.

Additions I do sometimes use are creamed horseradish (good with beef sausages), crème fraîche (in addition to milk for a creamy but not too creamy mash) and Parmesan, as in the following light, summery mash that makes a good companion to pork and leek sausages. The Luxury Mash is more akin to the French pomme purée – a richer, smoother mash with lashings of cream and butter and one that is particularly good with rich, winey sauces or gravies.

The Garlic & Olive Oil Mash is a useful recipe for the dairy-intolerant who need not be deprived of sausage and mash. (Personally, I think garlic works better in mash that's made with olive oil rather than butter).

PARMESAN & CHIVE MASH

900g potatoes, peeled and cut into
   even-sized pieces
50-60g grated Parmesan or Grano
   Padano cheese
2 heaped tbsp reduced fat crème fraîche
Salt and freshly ground black pepper

A small handful of chives, roughly chopped

SERVES 4

Put the potatoes in a pan of cold water, bring them up to the boil, add a little salt and cook them for about 20 minutes until just tender. Drain and mash the potatoes. Mix in the cheese, crème fraîche and most of the chives and season well with salt and freshly ground black pepper.

LUXURY MASH

800g red-skinned potatoes such as
   Desirée or Wilja
50ml double cream
75ml full cream milk
60-75g cubed, unsalted butter at room
   temperature
Salt and freshly ground black pepper
White truffle oil (optional)

SERVES 4

Peel the potatoes and cut them into largish cubes about 25g each (about half the size you would cut them for normal mash). Put them in a pan, pour over boiling water, add 1 tsp of salt and bring back to the boil. Turn down the heat and simmer gently for about 12-15 minutes until you can easily pierce them with a skewer. Drain them in a colander, then return them to the pan over a very low heat and leave them for a minute or two to dry off. Mix the cream and milk together and heat until just below boiling point in a microwave or separate saucepan. Tip the potatoes back into the colander then pass them through a potato ricer back into the pan. Pour in half the cream and beat with a wooden spoon, then gradually beat in the remaining cream and the butter. Season to taste with salt and freshly ground black pepper.

You could add a few drops of white truffle oil if you wanted to be exceptionally indulgent.

GARLIC & OLIVE OIL MASH

900g Desirée or other slightly waxy
   potatoes, peeled and halved or quartered
3 whole cloves of garlic, peeled
3-4 tbsp of extra virgin olive oil
   (depending how strong it is)
Salt and freshly ground black pepper

SERVES 4

Prepare the potatoes and boil them as described in Good, Everyday Mash (opposite), adding the whole cloves of garlic to the cooking water. When you drain the potatoes, reserve the cooking water. Fish out the garlic cloves and mash them separately on a saucer so you don't come across lumps of garlic in your mash. After you've done the initial mashing (with a potato masher or fork), add the mashed garlic, 3 tbsp of olive oil and 3 tbsp of the hot cooking water back to the mash and beat well. Add extra oil to intensify the flavour or more potato water if you want it slightly sloppier. Season well with salt and freshly ground black pepper. This mash goes well with Toulouse or other garlicky sausages.

You can use lemon or herb-flavoured oils to ring the changes on this mash. Basil-flavoured olive oil goes particularly well with Mediterranean-style sausages with sun-dried tomatoes. Lemony olive oil mash (which you can alternatively make by adding a couple of strips of lemon rind to the garlic with the boiling potatoes) suits Greek-style lamb and herb sausages.

MASH WITH ADDITIONS...

Although I'm not a big fan of flavoured mash, combinations of root vegetable purées and mashed potato work very well indeed.

CELERIAC & POTATO MASH

My favourite flavoured mash. This is a particularly good partner for venison and game sausages.

1 bulb of celeriac (about 500-600g)
A couple of pieces of lemon peel
Salt and freshly ground black pepper
An equal quantity of boiling potatoes
    (e.g. King Edwards)
3 tbsp extra virgin olive oil
1 heaped tbsp crème fraîche

SERVES 4

Give the celeriac a good scrub, then cut off the tough outer skin. The easiest way to do this is to prop it on a chopping board and cut downwards with a sharp knife.

Once you've got most of the skin off, cut it in quarters. Cut off any remaining bits of skin with a small knife. Cut into large cubes, put in a saucepan with a couple of bits of lemon peel and cover with boiling water. When it comes to the boil add salt then cook for about 15-20 minutes until soft. Drain well, reserving a little of the cooking water.

Peel the potatoes and cut them into equal-sized pieces. Cover with cold water, bring to the boil, add salt and cook until you can stick a knife through them without any resistance. Drain thoroughly and return to the pan to dry. Put the celeriac in a food processor and whizz until smooth, adding a little of the cooking water if it seems too dry and lumpy.

Mash the potato with a fork or masher until smooth. Add the oil and crème fraîche and beat well. Tip the puréed celeriac into the potato mash, mix well and season generously with salt and pepper.

COLCANNON

This famous Irish combination of mash and cabbage is not only celestial but practical. All your greens in one dish.

900g King Edwards or other good boiling
    potatoes, peeled and cubed
Sea salt and freshly ground black pepper
250g of sliced cabbage (you can now
    buy bags of sliced greens)
50g butter at room temperature
75ml warm milk

SERVES 4

Place the potatoes in a saucepan of cold water and bring to the boil. Skim off any froth, season with salt then cook for 20-25 minutes until done. Drain the potatoes thoroughly then return to the pan.

Meanwhile toss the greens for 2-3 minutes in a little boiling, salted water until just cooked. Drain, return to the pan and season with salt, pepper and 10g of the butter.

Mash the potatoes thoroughly till smooth, then beat in the remaining butter and milk. Season with salt and pepper then mix in the greens.

COLCANNON WITH LEEKS

I'm sure with leeks added this isn't strictly colcannon any more. But it's still very good.

Follow the preceding recipe for Colcannon, replacing the cabbage with two trimmed, washed, sliced leeks which you cook slowly in 40g of butter for 10 minutes then tip into your finished mash, once you've added the warm milk. Obviously, you don't need to add more butter to the mash. Or maybe you do.

BUBBLE & SQUEAK

Bubble and squeak is usually made from leftovers but is actually better if you cook the cabbagey element (which can be sprouts) from scratch.

About 500g each of cold boiled potatoes
   and cooked cabbage or sprouts
Salt and freshly ground black pepper
1 tbsp olive oil
25g butter

SERVES 4

Roughly chop up the potato and cabbage, mix together and season well with salt and pepper.

Heat a large frying pan over a moderate heat, add the oil, heat for a minute then add the butter. Tip in the potato and cabbage mix and flatten into a cake with a fork or a spatula. Let it cook for about 2-3 minutes then start to turn it over.

Keep turning it every few minutes until the crispy bits on the bottom of the pan get well mixed in to the hash – about 8-10 minutes in all. Good with almost any traditional pork sausage.

CRUSHED POTATOES WITH SPRING ONIONS

In the summer it's a struggle to make good mash, so give up and make crushed potatoes instead, which are equally scrummy. Oddly you don't seem to need as many potatoes as you do with mash. Maybe because the weather's warmer.

600g new potatoes, preferably Jerseys
Salt and freshly ground black pepper
2 tbsp olive oil
15g butter
5-6 spring onions, trimmed and roughly
  chopped or a small handful of chives

SERVES 4

Scrub the potatoes clean but don't peel them. Cut any larger ones in half or quarters, put them in a saucepan, cover with boiling water and bring the water back to the boil. Add salt and cook the potatoes until just tender (about 15 minutes) then drain and set aside.

Meanwhile heat a frying pan for a couple of minutes, add the oil, then the butter, then fry the spring onions or leeks for a couple of minutes until soft. Slice the potatoes thickly into the pan then mash roughly with a large fork. Fry, turning the potato for a couple of minutes, then season well with salt and pepper.

You can make a rather more glamourous Italian-style version of this with lemon, capers and parsley. Add the grated rind of half a lemon, 2 tbsp capers, rinsed and chopped and 3 tbsp finely chopped parsley to the potatoes once you've crushed them. Particularly good with chicken and asparagus sausages (see Simply Sausages, p152) and bratwurst.

VEGETABLE PURÉES

Vegetable purées are just as good as mash with sausages, and can also be a good option for carb-avoiders.

SILKY SWEDE & CARROT PURÉE

Silky and swede might sound like an unlikely juxtaposition of ideas but I promise you this fine-textured purée is elegant enough for a dinner party.

1 medium swede (about 500-550g) peeled and cut into small cubes
3 medium carrots (about 250-275g), peeled and sliced
1 litre hot vegetable stock made with 1 tbsp vegetable bouillon powder or an organic vegetable stock cube
25g butter
1 tbsp low-fat crème fraîche
Freshly ground black pepper plus a little grated nutmeg
Salt and lemon juice to taste

SERVES 4

Put the cubed swede and carrot in a medium sized saucepan and cover with the hot vegetable stock. Bring to the boil and simmer for about 20 minutes until the vegetables are soft. Strain, reserving the cooking water.

Put the vegetables in a food processor. Whizz them until smooth. Add the butter, crème fraîche and 1-2 tbsp of the vegetable cooking water and whizz again until smooth and silky. Season with plenty of black pepper, a little nutmeg and salt and/or lemon juice to taste.

Re-heat gently and serve with game sausages, haggis or white pudding.

SUMMER CARROT & CORIANDER PURÉE

The inspiration for this comes from a fantastic purée I tasted in a restaurant in the Loire region of France.
It goes particularly well with sausages with a touch of sweetness, such as pork and apricot or pork and apple.

A bunch of new carrots (about 500g – preferably organic)
2 tbsp olive oil
25g butter, cubed
2 shallots, peeled and roughly chopped
500ml hot vegetable stock made with 2 tsp vegetable bouillon powder or an organic vegetable stock cube
2 heaped tbsp of low-fat fromage frais
2 level tsp coriander seeds
Salt and pepper (preferably white) to taste

SERVES 4

Wash the carrots, scrubbing them if necessary, and slice into thin rounds. Put a large pan on to heat, add the olive oil, then the butter. Tip in the carrots and chopped shallots, stir well in the oil and butter mixture. Turn the heat right down, put a lid on the pan and cook the vegetables gently for about 10 minutes, stirring them occasionally so they don't catch. Pour in the hot stock, turn the

heat up and bring to the boil. Leaving the pan uncovered, simmer fast for about 15 minutes until the carrots are soft and the liquid has all but evaporated. Leave to cool for about 5 minutes.

Tip the carrots into a blender or food processor and whizz until smooth. Return the purée to the pan, re-heat it gently and stir in the fromage frais. Roughly grind the coriander seeds with a pestle and mortar and add to the purée. Season with salt and pepper to taste.

LEEK & PEA PURÉE

A sophisticated looking mash that belies its humble origins. The French are masters of instant mash, so use a product that's made in France rather than granules like Smash.

2 large leeks (about 500g)
2 tbsp olive oil
25g butter
85g frozen peas
1 level tsp organic vegetable bouillon
    powder
3-4 tbsp instant potato flakes
2 tbsp crème fraîche
Salt and pepper

SERVES 2-3

Cut the roots and about half the green tops off the leeks and strip off any damaged leaves. Cut vertically down each leek then rinse under running water, pulling the leaves aside so each layer gets well cleaned. Slice the leeks finely, then transfer to a colander and rinse again under running water. Heat a large pan for 2 minutes, add the oil, heat for a minute then add the butter. When the foaming dies down chuck in the leeks. Stir and put a lid over the pan and cook gently for 4-5 minutes until they begin to soften. Add the peas, the vegetable bouillon powder and 2 tbsp of water and stir. Replace the lid and simmer for another 7-8 minutes. Cool for a few minutes then tip the leeks and peas into a food processor or liquidiser and whizz until smooth. Return the purée to the saucepan, add the potato flakes and stir thoroughly, then add the crème fraîche. Re-heat gently over a low heat and season to taste with salt and pepper. This goes really well with light sausages such as chicken, bratwurst, the Veal, Lemon and Parsley Sausage on p144 or even a fish sausage.

PARSNIP & NUTMEG PURÉE

I am always amazed that the rather coarse-tasting parsnip can be transformed into such a sexy purée. Even parsnip-haters will love it.

4 medium sized parsnips (about 570g),
    preferably organic
Salt, pepper and freshly ground nutmeg
1-2 tbsp double cream

SERVES 4

Peel the parsnips and cut into even-sized cubes, cutting away the central woody core where necessary. Put in a saucepan, cover with boiling water, add a little salt and bring back to the boil. Cook for about 15 minutes until the parsnips are soft then drain them thoroughly, reserving the cooking water. Cool for a few minutes then whizz the parsnips in a food processor or blender until absolutely smooth.

Add 1 tbsp of the cream and 3-4 tbsp of the reserved cooking water until it looks seductively sloppy. Scoop it out of the food processor and back into the saucepan. Season with salt, pepper and freshly ground nutmeg. Add a little more cream or cooking water if you think it needs it and re-heat gently. Good with traditional pork sausages and with venison sausages too.

HESTON'S AMAZING CAULIFLOWER PURÉE

This fabulous-tasting dish comes from the brilliant Heston Blumenthal, the three Michelin-starred chef of the Fat Duck in Bray. He sieves it at the end which admittedly makes it even more sublime but if you're short of time or lack the inclination, it tastes great as it is.

1 medium to large cauliflower
85g unsalted butter
$1/4$ tsp best quality curry powder
175-200ml semi-skimmed milk
Salt and cayenne pepper

SERVES 4

Trim the base off the cauliflower, break into florets and chop them finely.

Place 75g of the butter in a large casserole and place on a medium to high heat. Add the cauliflower and cook, stirring occasionally until golden brown (about 12-15 minutes). Stir in the curry powder and cook for another five minutes, stirring until the cauliflower is nicely caramelised. Now add 150ml of the milk, and bring to the boil, stirring. Reduce the heat, cover the pan and simmer for 5 minutes.

Remove from the heat, leave to stand for 5 minutes, then tip into a liquidiser and purée. You may need a little extra milk at this stage.

Scoop the purée out of the blender and return to the pan. Whizz up the remaining milk in the blender to pick up the last bits of the purée and add as much of this milk as you need to the pan to get a soft, slightly sloppy consistency. Season with a fair amount of salt and a little cayenne pepper or chilli powder. Re-heat and serve.

This purée goes particularly well with a sweetish pork sausage, flavoured with apple or apricots and lightly buttered (or olive oiled) greens.

GRAVY

What makes good gravy? The kind you had as a kid is the answer for most of us. It also depends on which side of the channel you stand. For we Brits, it's a question of quantity. For the French, who aptly use the word 'jus', it's just a few spoonfuls. We favour onions and flour. The French and Italians base theirs on wine.

Sausagewise, I can't help but feel we've got it right. There can be booze (beer is good) but it must be diluted by an equal quantity of stock so the flavour is not too obvious.

The big problem is how to get it sufficiently meaty and savoury without juices from a roast to draw on. Certainly not from gravy granules which are an abomination. I'm also not massively keen on stock cubes or gravy browning. Amazingly the answer – unless you're into making home-made beef stock, and I do use proper stock when the recipe calls for it – is Marmite, which is far cheaper than the fresh stocks they now sell in cartons and surprisingly natural-tasting. Who'd have believed it?

A GOOD, SIMPLE ONION GRAVY

An easy, straightforward onion gravy to go with plain pork sausages and Good, Everyday Mash (*see* p24). The five spice powder, admittedly, is an unconventional departure but just gives the gravy an edge. Leave it out if you're a traditionalist and use Worcestershire Sauce instead.

1 tbsp olive oil or other cooking oil
20g butter
3 medium onions (about 300-350g), peeled and sliced
A small pinch of five spice powder (optional) or a few drops of Worcestershire sauce
1 rounded tbsp plain flour
350ml of stock made with boiling water and 1 tsp of Marmite
Freshly ground black pepper and a little salt if needed

SERVES 4

Heat a heavy saucepan or casserole over a moderate heat, add the oil, then, a few seconds later, the butter. Tip in the onions, stir well and cook over a medium heat for about 10 minutes until soft and beginning to brown. Stir in the five spice powder and flour and gradually add the hot stock, stirring it well as you go. Bring to the boil then turn the heat right down and simmer for 5 minutes or until ready to use it. Season with pepper to taste, a little salt if necessary and Worcestershire sauce if using.

To make this a bit ritzier you can add a slosh (3-4 tbsp) of dry Madeira or dry Marsala after you add the flour. To make it a bit sweeter add a tablespoon of tomato ketchup.

BEST EVER SAUSAGES WITH RICH GUINNESS GRAVY

My favourite sausage and gravy combination. For those of you new to the idea of cooking with Guinness, don't be put off – it actually makes the most fantastic dark, rich, sticky onion gravy that doesn't taste remotely of beer, and is perfect when served with a classic British Cumberland sausage. It also tastes really good made with plain Italian sausages (*see* p13).

2 tbsp olive oil
20g butter
2 large Spanish onions
 (about 425-450g), peeled and
 finely sliced
2 tsp golden granulated sugar
284 ml carton fresh beef stock
2 level tsp plain flour
250ml original Guinness
8 large traditional pork sausages or
 2 Cumberland rings (about 700g)
1 tbsp white wine vinegar
Sea salt

SERVES 4

Heat one tablespoon of the oil in a large frying pan, add the butter and, when it has melted, tip in the onions. Stir them so they're coated with the butter mixture, then cook slowly over a low heat for about 25-30 minutes until completely soft and quite brown. Sprinkle in the sugar and mix in well, then turn the heat up and stir continuously for about 5 minutes until the onions are really brown and caramelised.

Meanwhile, bring the stock to the boil and continue to boil rapidly until the volume is reduced by half (about 10 minutes). Stir the flour into the onions and cook for a minute, then add the stock and the Guinness. Bubble up for a minute or two then turn right down and leave to simmer.

Grill or fry the sausages, using the remaining oil, until browned on all sides.

Check the seasoning on the onion gravy adding salt, a tablespoon of white wine vinegar and a little water if it has got too thick. Transfer the sausages to the gravy, spooning it over them thoroughly, then continue to cook on a low heat for about 15-20 minutes until the sausages are cooked, adding extra water as needed. Serve with mashed potatoes or colcannon.

If you're not a big onion fan you can remove the sausages at the end of the cooking period and sieve the gravy.

You can use other beers for this – I suggest a robust British ale such as Marston's Pedigree or Coniston Bluebird.

SAUSAGE & CHIPS

Sausage and chips has such 'greasy spoon' connotations that you can forget what a great meal it is, made with really good sausages and hand cut chips. Add an egg if you're feeling specially indulgent. Get the sausages on first to leave you free to concentrate on the chips.

You may be surprised to learn that I cook my chips in a wok, but it's actually an ideal shape. You can move them around easily without any danger that hot oil will come up over the sides). Having said that I wouldn't make them for more than two people at a time as the temperature of the fat will drop and make your chips greasy.

So far as the ideal potato is concerned, Maris Piper is the variety that's most often recommended for chips but King Edwards will also do fine. Use an oil with a high frying point such as rapeseed or groundnut oil.

SAUSAGE & HANDCUT CHIPS WITH MALDON SEA SALT

4 of your favourite sausages
2 medium to large potatoes
  (about 350-375g)
About 350ml rapeseed oil
Maldon sea salt

SERVES 2

Peel the potatoes and cut them into quarters lengthways. Slice each quarter into 3 or 4 pieces then cut the fatter chips in half. Put the chips into a pan or bowl of cold water and give them a swirl, then take them out and dry them thoroughly in a clean tea towel.

Meanwhile, fill the wok about one third full of oil and heat over a medium to high heat for about four minutes. Drop a cube of bread into the oil when you think it looks about right; it should start to sizzle immediately. Using a shallow slotted spoon, gradually add the chips to the oil and fry for about 2-3 minutes until they are lightly cooked but not browned.

Remove them with the slotted spoon and place them in a bowl lined with kitchen paper. Give them a good shake to get rid of any excess oil. Heat the oil in the wok for another 2 minutes and then return the chips to the pan and fry for another 3 minutes until crisp and brown.

Drain again on kitchen towel and serve immediately, sprinkled with Maldon salt.

To zip up the chips grind a spice grinder over them along with the salt.

BLACK PUDDING WITH POTATO, APPLE & ONION PAN-FRY

At one time Northerners would have regarded this as a thoroughly effete and Southern way of serving black pudding but it's the kind of dish you now stumble across in any self-respecting gastropub. And it just happens to make a very nice supper for two.

2 medium sized potatoes (about 200g)
3/4 tbsp olive oil
1 small to medium sized onion
2 medium eating apples, e.g. Cox or
   Braeburn
A small handful of fresh sage leaves
Salt and pepper
A 250g pack of sliced black pudding or
   a small black pudding, thickly sliced

SERVES 2

Peel and halve the potatoes and cut them into thick slices. Tip into a bowl of cold water and swirl them around to get rid of some of the starch, then pat-dry with a clean tea towel.

Heat 2 tbsp of the oil in a frying pan, add the potatoes and fry for about 7-8 minutes, turning them over occasionally.

Meanwhile, peel and thinly slice the onion and quarter and slice the apples. Add the onions to the pan, season, stir and cook for a couple of minutes, then add the apple pieces and stir. Continue to cook, stirring and turning until all the ingredients are well browned and soft (about another 10 minutes), adding a little extra olive oil if it looks too dry. Add the sage for the last 5 minutes of the cooking time.

Meanwhile, heat the grill, rub the black pudding slices lightly with olive oil and cook them for about 4 minutes each side until hot and crispy. Lay them overlapping slightly on warm plates and spoon the potato and apple pan-fry alongside.

ALL-IN-ONE SAUSAGE ROAST

If you want a supper that calls for minimal effort but is really, really soothing and comforting make this.

450g new or waxy potatoes
2 medium red onions or other sweet
   onions (about 200g)
4-5 cloves of garlic or, even better in
   season, a head of 'wet' (i.e. fresh)
   garlic
3 tbsp olive oil
Salt and freshly ground black pepper
6 lamb and mint sausages or traditional
   pork sausages

SERVES 2

Pre-heat the oven to 200 C/400 F/Gas 6.

Scrub the potatoes clean but don't peel them. Cut them into chunky slices (about 4-5 cm thick). Peel and thickly slice the onions and garlic. Put them in a medium-sized roasting tin with 3 tbsp olive oil, season with salt and pepper and mix together well. Roast for 20 minutes, turn the potatoes and onions, then lay the sausages on top, turning them so they get a light coating of oil.

Cook for another 15 minutes, turn the sausages over then cook for a final 15-20 minutes. I don't think this is a dish that needs gravy but if you're a gravy addict feel free. I'd serve it with a classic French-style green salad (see below).

COS LETTUCE & CHIVE SALAD

I know we all use bagged salads these days but resist the temptation just for once and make a proper full-flavoured French green salad with a sharp, mustardy vinaigrette.

1 cos or sweet Romaine lettuce
1 level tsp Dijon mustard
Salt, pepper and (optionally) a small
   pinch of caster sugar
1 tbsp red or white wine vinegar
4 tbsp extra virgin olive oil
A small handful of chives
   (about $\frac{1}{2}$ a 20g pack)

SERVES 2

Cut through the base of the lettuce and tear off the coarser outer leaves. Wash the remaining leaves in cold water, tear them in two or three pieces then dry them in a salad spinner or a tea towel.

Whisk the mustard with the salt, pepper and red wine vinegar and gradually add the olive oil, whisking until you have a thick emulsion. Add 1-2 tablespoons of warm water to thin the dressing to a light

coating consistency and whisk again. Check the seasoning, adding a little sugar if you find it too sharp.

Just before serving, put the leaves in a bowl and toss with the dressing. Cut the chives across 3 or 4 times with scissors (to make longish pieces) and scatter them over the top of the salad. Toss the leaves again and serve.

CHINESE-STYLE SAUSAGES WITH STIR-FRIED GREENS

I was dying to use Chinese sausages somewhere in the book but discovered that they were a) fiendishly difficult to track down and b) more like pepperami than a fresh sausage. Then I hit on the idea of jazzing up chipolatas in a Chinese style, which really tastes enticingly exotic. The ideal recipe for carb-avoiders.

2 heads of spring greens or spring
  cabbage or a pack of sliced greens
1 bunch of spring onions
1½ tbsp sunflower oil or other light
  cooking oil
450g of chipolata sausages
1 large clove of garlic, crushed
1 tbsp light soy sauce
3 tbsp hoi sin sauce mixed with 3 tbsp
  water
1 tbsp toasted sesame seeds
  (see footnote)

SERVES 2-3

Pick the outer, darker leaves off the greens or cabbage and wash well. With a sharp knife, cut away the central rib of each leaf then roll it up and slice it into ribbons, to give you about 300g of greens. (You can use the rest in another dish.) Trim the spring onions and cut lengthways into halves or quarters, then across into thirds to give you long, thin shreds.

Heat the oil in a wok and stir-fry the onions briefly for a minute. Scoop them out with a slotted spoon then turn the heat down slightly and fry the sausages for about 6-7 minutes, turning them so they brown evenly. Remove them from the pan and pour off all but 1 tbsp of the oil. Turn the heat up again and stir-fry the greens for a couple of minutes, adding the crushed garlic, soy sauce and a tablespoon of water half way through.

Put the greens in serving bowls. Return the sausages to the pan, pour in the hoi sin sauce and water, and bubble up until the sauce is reduced and sticky. Tip back the spring onions, stir, then spoon the sausages and onions over the greens. Sprinkle over the sesame seeds and serve. You could also serve some plain boiled rice with this.

To toast sesame seeds, simply heat them in a dry pan over a moderate heat, stirring them from time to time until they start to release a nutty aroma and turn pale gold.

66 PASTA
74 PIZZA
78 PIES
84 TOAD IN THE HOLE

PASTA, PIZZA & PIES

SPAGHETTI WITH MEATBALLS

I don't know why but Spaghetti with Meatballs always seems much sexier than Spaghetti Bolognese. Maybe it's the Italian-American connection, the idea of some cosy, New York neighbourhood trattoria still firmly stuck in the fifties. Anyway, it's a really easy and enjoyable dish to make. Sausage meat gives meatballs a particularly smooth texture.

400g plain, traditional pork sausages without herbs
500g minced beef or veal
2 large cloves of garlic, peeled and crushed
2 tbsp finely chopped flat leaf parsley
50g fresh breadcrumbs
2 tbsp milk
Salt and freshly ground black pepper
Plain flour for shaping
4 tbsp olive oil
150ml dry Italian white wine
400g can of chopped tomatoes
450g fresh tomatoes, peeled and roughly chopped
600g spaghetti
A handful of basil leaves or extra chopped parsley

SERVES 6

Slit the sausage casings and slip them off the sausages. Put the sausage meat in a bowl with the minced beef or veal. Add the garlic, parsley, breadcrumbs and milk and mix everything together thoroughly. Season with salt and pepper and mix again.

Sprinkle a chopping board with flour and flour your hands. Scoop out spoonfuls of the meat mixture and shape them into meatballs roughly the size of a large walnut.

Heat 3 tbsp of the oil in a large frying pan and cook the meatballs in batches, browning them on all sides. Put them in a large casserole or pan (try to get them in a single layer). When you've fried all the meatballs, pour off any excess fat and de-glaze the pan with the white wine.

Add the chopped tinned and fresh tomatoes, season with salt and pepper, cook for a couple of minutes then pour over the meatballs. Partially cover the pan and cook the meatballs over a low heat for about half an hour, spooning over the sauce occasionally.

About 15 minutes before the end of the cooking time start cooking the spaghetti in a large pan of boiling salted water, following the cooking time recommended on the pack. When it's al dente (i.e. still has some 'bite') drain it and return it to the pan. Add the remaining oil and toss well. Just before serving, roughly tear the basil leaves and stir them (or the extra parsley) into the tomato sauce. Serve the spaghetti in individual bowls, spooning the meatballs and sauce over the top.

SICILIAN SAUSAGE PASTA WITH CAPERS, OLIVES & FETA

A really gutsy pasta dish for lovers of strong flavours. Note the recipe doesn't use any salt – you don't need it with the capers, olives and Feta, all of which add their own saltiness to the dish.

400g garlic and chilli-flavoured sausages
1 tbsp olive oil
2 level tbsp tomato paste
125ml white wine
1/2 a 400g tin pomodorino cherry
    tomatoes
2 tbsp capers, well rinsed
10-12 green or black olives, pitted and
    roughly chopped
300g dried rigatoni or penne
Cajun-style spice grind
20g pack parsley, finely chopped
100g Feta cheese

SERVES 3-4

Using a small sharp knife, cut a slit in the sausage skins and peel them off. Heat the oil in a large frying pan and add the sausages, breaking them up as you go with a wooden spoon. Add the tomato paste, stir in well and fry for a minute or two. Add the white wine, let it bubble up then add the cherry tomatoes. Break them down with a fork, together with any larger pieces of sausage meat. Add the capers and olives, stir, then leave to simmer for about 15 minutes.

Meanwhile, boil the pasta in salted water until just cooked, spooning off 2-3 tablespoons of the cooking water into the pasta sauce. Drain the pasta and return it to the pan.

Check the seasoning in the sauce, adding a little Cajun spice to taste, then pour over the pasta. Add half the parsley, toss together and leave to stand for a couple of minutes for the flavours to amalgamate. Break up the Feta cheese roughly with a fork. Spoon the pasta onto warm plates, crumble over some Feta and a sprinkling of parsley and serve with additional Cajun spice on the table.

QUICK GARLIC & FENNEL SAUSAGE PIZZA

If you're not into making your own pizza dough, but want to produce one that looks home-made, try this really easy recipe – also a great recipe to use any leftover sausages in the unlikely event that you have any.

A small (250g) microwaveable pack of spinach leaves (optional)
5-6 tbsp passata or Easy Tomato Sauce (see below)
2 medium to large plain naan breads or 4 smaller ones
A little olive oil
Freshly ground black pepper
400g finely cooked Italian garlic and fennel sausages or other garlicky sausages (e.g. Sicilian, Toulouse), sliced diagonally into four
100g Taleggio or Fontina cheese, rind removed and thinly sliced

Microwave the spinach following the instructions on the pack. Drain well and set aside. Warm up the passata or tomato sauce.

Pre-heat the grill on a medium setting and grill the base of the naan pizzas until just crisp. Turn them over and spread with the tomato sauce. Divide the spinach between the two pizzas, trickle over a little olive oil and season with black pepper.

Put a layer of sliced sausage on each pizza and top with the thinly sliced cheese. Replace under the grill, and cook until the sausage begins to sizzle and the cheese has melted (about 4-5 minutes).

If you're using cold sausages rather than recently cooked ones, fry the slices lightly on each side to warm them through before you use them to top the pizza.

SERVES 2-4

EASY TOMATO SAUCE

2 tbsp olive oil
1 clove of garlic, peeled and crushed
1 x 400g tin of tomatoes
Salt, pepper and sugar to taste

Heat the oil in a large frying pan. Add the garlic. Tip in the tin of tomatoes and crush with a fork or a wooden spoon.

Season with salt, pepper and a pinch of sugar and simmer for about 10 minutes until the sauce is thick and jammy.

SAUSAGE, ONION & APPLE PIE

In my opinion you can never have too many pie recipes, and this homely West country-inspired version is a real winner. It's the kind of dish they should serve in pubs, if they weren't so busy dishing out seared tuna and rocket.

4 tbsp light olive oil or sunflower oil
8 good quality plain pork sausages (about 550g in total)
2 medium onions, peeled and roughly sliced
2 medium carrots, peeled and thinly sliced
1 large Bramley apple (about 250g) or 2 medium Cox's or Blenheim apples, peeled and roughly chopped
1 level tsp ground coriander
1 heaped tbsp plain flour
$\frac{1}{2}$ tsp fresh thyme leaves
200ml dry cider
200ml light vegetable or chicken stock
500g ready-made puff pastry
1 beaten egg

SERVES 4-5

Heat a large, deep frying pan or casserole, add 1 tbsp of the oil and fry the sausages on all sides until lightly browned. Set the sausages aside and discard the fat in the pan.

Give the pan a wipe, then add the remaining oil, and fry the onions and carrots gently for about five minutes until beginning to soften. Add the apples and cook for a further 3-4 minutes, then stir in the ground coriander and flour. Stir in the cider, stock and thyme, bring to the boil and then simmer for about 10 minutes until the onions and carrots are almost cooked. Check and adjust the seasoning if necessary.

Cut each sausage diagonally into three and put in a shallow pie dish. Pour over the onion and apple sauce and leave to cool. Pre-heat the oven to 220 C/425 F/ Gas 7.

Roll out the puff pastry thickly, and cut a circle just wider than the circumference of the dish. Roll out the offcuts and cut a series of narrow strips to line the edge of the pie dish. Dampen the edge of the dish and arrange the strips around the edge, then dampen the top edge of the strips. Lower the pastry lid down on top of the edge of the pie, press down lightly and trim the overhanging pastry off the edge of the pie. With the back of a small knife indent the edge of the pastry at regular intervals. Paint the top of the pie with the egg glaze. Roll out the remaining pastry and cut it into decorative shapes. Decorate the pie then glaze them too.

Bake in the pre-heated oven for 20 minutes, then turn the heat down to 190 C/375 F/Gas 5 for a further 25-30 minutes until the pastry is well browned. Serve with some buttered greens.

MINI SAUSAGE TOADS

Somehow this recipe creates the illusion that it's not really as fattening as a full-blown toad. Which is, of course, totally untrue. But it looks cute and is perfect for a family meal with small children. Or even large children.

110g plain flour
$1/4$ level tsp salt
2 medium eggs or 1 large egg, lightly beaten
175ml semi-skimmed milk mixed with 125ml water
6 large traditional pork sausages (about 450g)
3-4 tbsp of vegetable oil

You will need a deep 12 hole muffin tin

SERVES 6

Sift the flour into a large bowl and sprinkle over the salt. Make a hollow in the centre of the flour and add the egg and about a quarter of the milk and water mix. Gradually work the flour into the egg with a wooden spoon until it is all incorporated, beating it briskly until smooth. Now gradually add the rest of the milk, beating well between each addition. Pour the batter into a jug and leave in the fridge for at least 30 minutes while you get the oven and pan ready.

Heat the oven to 225 C/425 F/Gas 7. Pour a little oil into the bottom of each hole in the muffin pan then heat the pan in the oven till the oil is smoking hot (about 10-12 minutes).

Meanwhile, heat a pan, add the remaining oil and brown the sausages lightly on all sides. Cut them in half. Take the tin out of the oven, put a half sausage in each hole in the pan, and pour the batter around them. (It should immediately start to bubble up and sizzle.) Put the pan back in the oven and cook for 25 minutes until the puddings are well browned and puffed up.
Serve immediately with peas or baked beans.

90 RICE
96 BEANS
102 GRAINS

RICE, BEANS & GRAINS

ITALIAN SAUSAGE, TOMATO & BASIL RISOTTO

Surprisingly, using sausage in a risotto is perfectly respectable. The Italians have many risotti con salsiccie. The sausage meat gets taken out of its skin, broken up, fried and then added to the rice along with the other ingredients to make a really tasty, hearty, rustic dish.

300g fresh Italian sausages
$1/2$ tsp ground fennel seeds
3 tbsp olive oil
225g risotto rice (Arborio or Carnaroli)
100g fresh or frozen peas (optional)
1 medium to large onion (about 150g),
   peeled and finely chopped
A small (200g) tin of premium Italian plum
   tomatoes or $1/2$ a 400g tin
$2/3$ of a glass of dry white wine (about
   100ml) plus 3 tbsp to finish the dish
1 litre of good home-made or bought
   fresh chicken stock
2 tbsp freshly grated Parmesan
A small (20g) pack of basil leaves
   or 20 large basil leaves
Salt and pepper

SERVES 4

Slit the skins of the sausages and peel away. Heat a large heavy saucepan or casserole and add 1 tbsp of olive oil. Fry the sausage meat with the fennel seeds until lightly browned, breaking it down with a wooden spoon, then remove it with a slotted spoon and set it aside.

Add the remaining olive oil, turn down the heat and fry the onion gently for about 4 minutes until beginning to soften.

Heat the stock to boiling point in a saucepan and leave it over a low heat to simmer. Tip the rice into the onion, stir and cook for 3 minutes, stirring occasionally to make sure it doesn't catch and burn.

Return the sausage to the pan along with the peas, if using, and the tomatoes, breaking them up with your spoon. Pour in the white wine and let it bubble up and evaporate. Add the hot stock to the rice with a ladle or cup, a ladleful at a time, stirring until each addition is absorbed. You may not need all the stock but carry on until the rice is soft but still has a tiny bit of a bite (about 20 minutes in all). Turn off the heat, stir in the Parmesan and season to taste with salt and black pepper.

Cover the pan for 5 minutes and leave the risotto to rest. Spoon the risotto into bowls and top with the torn basil leaves (about 5 to a bowl).

THAI SAUSAGES WITH LEEK & LEMONGRASS RICE

What to eat with Thai sausages? Mash doesn't work, noodles are too slithery. But this refreshing, lightly spiced rice is perfect.

8 Thai-flavoured sausages
1½ tbsp sunflower oil or light olive oil

For the rice
2 medium leeks
2 tbsp sunflower oil or light olive oil
1 tsp ginger and garlic paste (available
　　from Asian shops)
175g Thai jasmine rice or Basmatti rice
350 ml hot lemongrass stock
　　(see footnote)
1 tsp fish sauce or salt to taste

SERVES 4

Trim the roots and the top half of the green leaves off the leeks. Cut down the centre of the leek almost to the root and wash any dirt away under cold running water, pulling the leaves apart. Finely slice the leeks and set aside the greenest leaves. Rinse again.

Heat the oil in a heavy saucepan or casserole, add the leeks (except the green bits) and stir. Cook for a couple of minutes until beginning to soften then stir in the ginger and garlic paste and the jasmine rice. Pour in the stock, bring to the boil then turn the heat down, cover and simmer until all the liquid has been absorbed (about 15 minutes).

Meanwhile, fry the sausages in a little oil until nicely browned (about 15-20 minutes – see p16). Add the remaining leek leaves and the fish sauce or salt to the rice and fork it through to fluff it up. Replace the lid and steam for another 5 minutes and serve with the sausages.

It's important to buy leeks with some flavour for this dish – either organic or locally grown.

To make the lemongrass stock, put 2 sticks of lemongrass or 1 rounded tbsp dried lemongrass in a measuring jug with 1 rounded tsp of Marigold (or other good quality) vegetable bouillon powder and pour over boiling water to the 350ml mark. Cover and leave to infuse for 20-30 minutes.

SAUSAGE CHILLI

This recipe may sound a bit cheesy but actually it works brilliantly. And my entire family loves it. What more could a mother want?

250g pack dried black beans or kidney
   beans, soaked overnight, or, if you're
   short of time, 2 x 400g cans
1 green pepper
5 tbsp sunflower or olive oil
2 medium onions, peeled and roughly
   chopped
2 large cloves of garlic, peeled and
   crushed
2 level tsp mild chilli powder
$\frac{1}{2}$ rounded tsp cumin powder (optional)
1 x 400g tin whole or chopped tomatoes
400g spicy beef or pork sausages
   (e.g. with Cajun-style seasoning)
Salt
3 heaped tbsp fresh coriander

SERVES 4

Having soaked the beans overnight, put them on to cook following the instructions on the pack.

Meanwhile, wash the pepper, cut into quarters, slice away the white pith and seeds and cut into chunks. Heat 3 tbsp of the oil in a large saucepan, add the onion and pepper and cook for about 5-6 minutes until beginning to soften. Add the chopped garlic, the chilli powder and cumin, if using, stir, cook for a minute then add the tomatoes and stir again. Turn the heat down, cover and leave to simmer slowly while the beans carry on cooking. (Or for about 15 minutes if using canned beans).

Brown the sausages on all sides in the remaining oil and cut diagonally into three. Drain the beans. Add the beans and the sausages to the tomato mixture. Stir, replace the lid and cook for another 10-15 minutes to let the flavours amalgamate. Just before serving, check the seasoning, adding salt to taste, if necessary, and stir in the fresh coriander. Serve with warm tortillas and a sharply dressed green salad.

TOULOUSE SAUSAGES WITH PUY LENTILS

The earthy flavour of lentils acts as a fantastic foil to French-style sausages – and Puy lentils are the best. A classic French bistro meal.

8 Toulouse sausages or other garlicky
   sausages
1$\frac{1}{2}$ tbsp light olive oil

For the lentils
175g Puy lentils
1 medium carrot, peeled and chopped
   into small dice
550ml vegetable stock, made with 2
   rounded tsp vegetable bouillon powder
   or an organic vegetable stock cube
3 tbsp olive oil
3 cloves of garlic, peeled and finely sliced
1 medium to large onion, peeled and
   roughly chopped
$\frac{1}{2}$ tsp sweet Spanish paprika (pimenton)
2 heaped tbsp chopped flat leaf parsley
Salt and freshly ground pepper to taste

SERVES 4

Rinse the lentils and put them in a pan with the chopped carrots and stock. Bring to the boil and simmer for 20-25 minutes until the liquid has evaporated.

Heat 2 tbsp of the oil in a pan over a low heat, add the sliced garlic and let it cook gently for a couple of minutes until beginning to colour. Add the onion, stir and cover the pan and leave to cook slowly until the lentils are ready.

Stir the paprika into the onions and cook for a minute then tip in the lentils, stir well, cover and leave over a very low heat while you cook the sausages (*see* p17). Season the lentils with salt and pepper to taste, then stir in the chopped parsley and remaining olive oil. Serve with the sausages and a green salad.

MERGUEZ WITH WARM COUSCOUS SALAD & HARISSA DRESSING

Merguez is a wonderfully spicy North African lamb sausage that's hugely popular in France.
The best ones are the long thin ones. I have no idea why. They just don't seem to work very well as a fat sausage.

About 600g Merguez or other spicy
   sausages
2 tbsp light cooking oil

For the salad
2 large or 3 medium courgettes
   (about 300g)
1 medium red pepper
1 medium onion, peeled and chopped
4 tbsp olive oil
300ml stock made with 1 rounded tsp
   vegetable bouillon powder
200g instant couscous
2 tsp Moroccan spice mix (see below)
2 heaped tbsp finely chopped coriander
   plus 1 heaped tbsp finely chopped
   mint
Salt and lemon juice to taste

For the harissa dressing
2 tsp harissa paste
A pinch of cinnamon

SERVES 4

Heat 2 tbsp of oil in a frying pan and put the sausages on to cook over a low heat, turning them occasionally.

Meanwhile, slice the ends off the courgettes and cut them in three or four lengthways, then across into cubes. Quarter and de-seed the pepper then cut it into similar sized pieces. Heat a large frying pan, add the oil and heat for a minute then tip in the courgettes, pepper and onions. Stir-fry over a low to moderate heat for about 10 minutes until soft and browned.

Make up the couscous by measuring it into a bowl. Pour over just over 200ml of the hot stock. Stir, cover the bowl and leave the couscous to absorb the liquid for about 4 minutes, then fluff up the grain with a fork. Sprinkle the spice mix over the vegetables and stir in. Turn off the heat, tip the couscous and herbs into the frying pan and fork them through, so that they are evenly distributed. Season with salt, pepper and a squeeze of lemon juice.

Mix the harissa paste with the remaining stock and season with a little cinnamon and salt if needed. Serve the sausages with the couscous salad and a spoonful of harissa sauce drizzled over them. A dark green salad such as spinach, watercress and rocket goes well with this.

Moroccan spice mix is a mild, aromatic blend that I use regularly for recipes. Make up a batch from 2 tbsp ground cumin, 2 tbsp ground coriander, 1 tbsp turmeric and 1-2 tsp hot (piccante) Spanish pimenton or chilli powder. Blend well and use as desired (about 2 tsp at a time).

110 BREAKFAST
116 HOT DOG HEAVEN
120 PICNICS
126 BARBECUES
130 SALSAS
132 OTHER SNACKS
136 CHRISTMAS

FEASTS

BREAKFAST

I'm a total traditionalist when it comes to breakfast. Other times of the day I'm happy to eat sausages seasoned with garlic, chilli or fennel seeds, but before 12 noon it's got to be just white pepper and mace. I'm agnostic on herbs. They can be a little bit herby but not aggressively so.

You also don't want your breakfast sausage to take too long, which is why I prefer chipolatas. A good butcher's one, for preference, not least because we all ought to do our bit to keep the few remaining independents in business.

A running order is important with fry-ups. Sausage, then bacon and tomato and finally egg. Separate pans if you're cooking mushrooms otherwise everything turns a dirty grey.

Indulgences like the Cashel Blue & Bacon Potato Cakes overleaf or black pudding are for weekend brunches only. Kidneys are an occasional Edwardian extravagance and very good with sausages (you might as well devil them while you're at it).

A better summer option is a breakfast bap or sausage panini, a slightly pointless exercise in some ways when you can simply have a fry up and bread or toast, but there is something wantonly seductive about squishing your entire breakfast in a roll. And there's always the smug satisfaction of being able to cook it better than the local station cafeteria.

This is also the moment for the classic sausage sandwich, which should be made with thickly cut slices from a freshly baked white loaf (not sliced bread), spread with soft butter and maybe the merest whisper of English (not Dijon) mustard. No ketchup, so far as I'm concerned anyway.

CASHEL BLUE & BACON POTATO CAKES

This is a rather ritzy version of the Irish potato cake, but I like the salty and savoury notes it brings to the feast. Theoretically the recipe makes enough for eight but you'll find four will easily demolish them. Or you can freeze a few.

700g King Edward or other boiling
   potatoes, peeled and halved or
   quartered
1 tbsp cooking oil
75g lean rindless streaky bacon,
   cut with scissors into very small pieces
15g butter
1/2 bunch of spring onions (about 4 onions),
   trimmed and finely sliced
110g plain flour plus extra for dusting
   the cakes
1 egg yolk
110g Cashel Blue or Stilton cheese
Salt and freshly ground pepper

MAKES 8 WEDGES

Put the potatoes in a saucepan of cold water, bring them to the boil, add a little salt and cook for about 20 minutes till tender.

Meanwhile, heat a small frying pan for a couple of minutes on the hob, add the oil and fry the bacon until the fat starts to run and it begins to brown (about 3 minutes). Add the butter and the sliced spring onions, stir-fry for a minute then take off the heat and set aside.

When the potatoes are cooked, drain them in a colander then return them to the pan for a minute over a low heat to dry them out thoroughly. Break them up and mash them with a fork until they're completely smooth, then leave to cool for 10 minutes or so. When cool, work in the flour, egg yolk, onions and bacon, season with salt and freshly ground black pepper and leave until almost cold. Break the cheese up well with a fork and mix into the mash.

Generously flour a chopping board and form the mash into a flat cake about 1½ cm deep. Cut it into 8 wedges, flour them lightly and lay out on a baking tray and put in the fridge for at least an hour (or overnight).

To cook the potato cakes, heat a heavy frying pan until quite hot, add a little oil and wipe away the surplus with kitchen towel. Lightly dust the potato cakes again with a little more flour and cook for about 4 minutes each side until well browned and you can see the cheese beginning to ooze temptingly from the centre.

Rather than making mash specially for the potato cakes you could make extra when you're cooking sausage and mash, but don't add milk or butter, and use it while it's still lukewarm rather than once it's gone cold and hard.

SAUSAGE, EGG & BACON PANINI

Have you noticed how the word panini has crept onto menus everywhere? It sounds so much swankier than a roll. I'm always buying them at stations and airports and then wishing I hadn't. You can make a much better one at home. If you have a contact (electric, double-sided) grill or a George Foreman Lean Mean Grilling Machine (for which high calorie feasts I'm sure it wasn't designed), try it.

2 tbsp sunflower oil or other light
   cooking oil
2 chipolata sausages
2 thin slices of streaky bacon
1 medium egg
1 panini roll or 1/3 of a large ciabatta
Olive oil spray
Tomato ketchup (optional)

SERVES 1

Pre-heat a contact grill. Heat a medium-sized frying pan, add the oil then fry the sausages for about 10-12 minutes until brown and well cooked. Remove from the pan, add the bacon and then break in an egg, pushing the white in towards the centre to make it as compact as possible.

Split the roll or ciabatta and spray both sides with olive oil. Toast the cut sides on the grill without putting the lid down.

Turn the bottom half of the roll over, cut the sausages in half lengthways and lay them on top – or as much of them as you can fit in a single layer (eat the rest). Place the bacon on top, then the egg and a good squirt of ketchup. Press the top half of the roll on the filling then press the lid down lightly but firmly. Cook for about a minute to a minute and a half until the crust is crisp and beginning to brown. Serve with more ketchup or mustard.

SAUSAGE, EGG & BACON BAPS

If you can't be bothered to faff around with the grill, simply stuff the sausage, bacon and egg into a large buttered or unbuttered bap and ketchup as above.

MODERN MIXED GRILL

Actually, not that modern. Or grilled come to that. But an attempt to introduce some vegetables into the classic fry-up.
A great brunch dish.

2 tbsp olive oil
10g butter, plus extra for the beans
1 Cumberland sausage ring
 (about 175g)
2 thick slices of black pudding
4 thick slices smoked streaky bacon,
 de-rinded
125g cherry tomatoes
125g podded broad beans, fresh or
 frozen
A small handful or a small pack of rocket
 or watercress

SERVES 2

Heat a large pan, add the oil and then the butter. Brown the sausage on both sides. Cook the black pudding and fry the streaky bacon until crisp, then remove them as they cook and keep warm. Toss the cherry tomatoes in the hot oil. Cook the beans in a little salted water until tender (about 4 minutes), drain and add a knob of butter. Arrange a few rocket leaves on each plate and top with the hot tomatoes.

Serve the sausage, black pudding and bacon alongside, together with a helping of beans.

DEVILLED KIDNEYS

A favourite item on the Edwardian breakfast table which goes really well with a breakfast sausage.
This is a dish only worth making with the freshest of kidneys from your local butcher. Adjust the spicing to taste –
they should be piquant but not overbearingly hot.

8 lambs kidneys in suet
1 heaped tbsp plain flour (about 20g)
1-1 $\frac{1}{2}$ tsp Colman's English Mustard
 Powder
$\frac{1}{2}$-1 tsp hot Spanish pimenton or chilli
 powder (less if you use the latter)
2 tbsp sunflower oil or other light
 cooking oil
75ml beef stock or stock made with
 $\frac{1}{2}$ tsp Marmite (see page 34)
2 tsp Worcestershire sauce plus extra
 for serving
10g butter (optional)
Freshly ground black pepper

SERVES 4

Strip the suet off the kidneys, cut them in half lengthways and snip away the central white core (easiest with scissors). Pull the outer skin off the kidneys.

Mix together the flour, mustard powder and pimenton or chilli powder, and dip the kidneys in the mix.

Heat a large frying pan and add the oil. Lay the kidneys in the pan and fry until blood appears on the surface (about 2 minutes). Turn them over and cook

the other side for another 2 minutes, then turn them once more and cook for another minute.

Pour 3 tbsp of stock into the pan and let it sizzle up, then add the Worcestershire sauce. Check the seasoning adding pepper and a little extra mustard or pimenton if you think it needs it (it shouldn't need salt but add some if you wish). Add a knob of butter and a little extra stock and serve with sausages and scrambled eggs or sausages, fried tomatoes and watercress.

HOT DOG HEAVEN

What is it about hot dogs that makes everyone come over all misty-eyed? 'Mmmmm, hot dogs' my eldest daughter murmured dreamily when I announced I was going to test them. 'Yesssss!' whooped our photographer, Georgia. Which is weird when you think they come down to a mass produced frank (in this country at least), a soggy white roll and some, gloopy, over-sweetened tomato ketchup. But by the time I'd run those dogs through their paces, American style, inspired by an hour's browsing on the web, I got the point.

Americans apparently eat over 2 billion of them in July alone according to the ultimate hot dog oracle www.hot-dog.com, the website of the National Hot Dog and Sausage Council, and every region – even individual cities – have their own variation. Here are some you can try, but first a few words about two all-important subjects: the Sausage and the Bun.

THE SAUSAGE

Must be a frankfurter, 'frank' for short. I've tried them with traditional English sausages and it's just not the same. Ideally they should be barbecued, but a ridged grill pan creates a similar effect.

Pat them dry when you take them out of the packet and roll them lightly in sunflower oil. How long they'll take depends on how fat they are. The standard supermarket frank will cook in about 3 minutes. A superior German-style frank (available from food halls such as Selfridges and specialist delis) will take about 6-8 minutes.

THE BUN

Should be soft but not soggy. Slightly crusty but not hard. The best place to find them is an independent baker. You want a long, deep roll about 12cm long and 7-8 cm deep (not that you're actually going to measure it). A supermarket finger roll is too soft. You're better off with what they call a 'French roll' which is like a mini baguette, only softer and fatter.

There are two schools of thought about whether to toast it. Some like to open it up and give the inside a minute or so on the barbecue. Others prefer it just soft, split and filled. Either way, don't cut right through it but leave a hinge on the side.

VERY GOOD SCOTCH – OR MAYBE WELSH – EGGS

Home-made Scotch eggs are in a different league from the lurid orange-crumbed rubbery objects you find in petrol stations. Now that you can get every flavour of sausage under the sun, you can also ring the changes. Here I've made them with leek sausages (hence the feeling that they should be Welsh rather than Scotch) but you could try other flavours too.

6 large fresh free-range eggs, preferably organic plus an extra large or medium egg
2 x 400g packs pork and leek sausages or premium pork sausages plus 2 rounded tbsp finely chopped chives
Plain flour
About 60g natural breadcrumbs
Corn or rapeseed oil for frying

SERVES 6

Pour a large kettle of boiling water into a saucepan and bring back to the boil. Gently lower 6 of the eggs into the water, bring back to the boil and boil for 10 minutes. Drain the water away, pour cold water over the eggs to arrest the cooking process and leave to cool.

Snip the casings of the sausages and pull them off. Tip the sausage meat into a large bowl and mash with a fork. If you're using ordinary sausages, add the chopped chives at this point. Divide the mixture into six portions.

When the eggs are cool, crack them on a hard surface and then peel away the shells under cold running water. Pat them dry with kitchen towel.

Sprinkle a little flour on a chopping board and lightly flour your hands. Take one portion of the sausage meat and press it into a flat disc and wrap it round one of the eggs pressing the mixture together so that there aren't any cracks. Lightly roll the sausage-covered egg in flour and set aside, then repeat with the remaining 5 eggs.

Break the other egg into a shallow dish, add a teaspoon of water and whisk lightly with a fork. Pour half the breadcrumbs into another dish. Dip the eggs one by one into the egg mixture, then press into the breadcrumbs making sure the egg is thoroughly coated. Set aside as you do them.

Heat a wok over a moderate heat for about 2 minutes then pour in a couple of centimetres of oil and heat again. Carefully lower three of the eggs into the hot oil and fry, turning them over every minute or so, until the outside is evenly browned and the sausage meat fully cooked. This should take about 8-10 minutes – you may need to turn down the heat slightly if they appear to be cooking too fast. Repeat with the remaining eggs, replacing the oil with clean oil if it looks a bit yukky.

Drain the Scotch eggs on some kitchen towel then leave on a plate to cool for at least an hour. Halve and serve with a potato salad such as the New Potato, Broad Bean and Herb Salad on p57 or just a simple, crisp lettuce salad.

CHORIZO, MORCILLA & PEPPER KEBABS

You might wonder why bother to turn a sausage into a kebab when you can simply plonk it straight on the grill. There isn't any good reason apart from the fact that it looks great, especially with the dramatic red and black of authentic Spanish chorizo and morcilla sausages (*see* p13). You will need 8 metal skewers for this recipe.

4-5 fresh chorizo sausages (not the dried kind for slicing) – about 400g
3-4 morcilla sausages or about 400g sliced black pudding
2 large red ramiro peppers or ordinary red peppers, quartered, de-seeded and cut into squares
2 red onions, peeled and quartered
Aerosol olive oil spray
Salt and pepper
8 wheat or corn tortillas

SERVES 4-8

Cut the sausages apart. Cut the smaller ones into four and the bigger ones into 5 slices. Or cut the black pudding slices into four. Separate out the onion pieces and the squares of red pepper.
Thread up the two sausages on the skewers, starting with a piece of onion and pepper, then a piece of morcilla or chorizo, more onion and pepper then a slice of the other sausage and so on – about 5 pieces of sausage per skewer. Don't pack them too tightly – they won't cook as well. Just before cooking them, spray each skewer lightly with oil and

season with salt and pepper then cook over moderately hot coals (see footnote) for about 8-10 minutes turning the skewers at least a couple of times. If they seem to be cooking too quickly move them to the outer edges of the barbecue away from the direct heat. Pull the meat off the skewers and stuff into warm tortillas. Serve with guacamole and Pico de Gallo salsa (see below and over).

It's best to cook the kebabs once the initial blast of heat has died down from the barbecue to prevent flare-ups.

AUTHENTIC ROUGH-CRUSHED GUACAMOLE

Guacamole needs a bit of texture. This is the way the Mexicans make it.

3 medium-sized ripe avocados
Juice of a lime
1/2 a white or red onion (about 75g) finely chopped
1 small green chilli, deseeded and finely chopped
1 large clove of garlic, peeled and crushed with 1/4 tsp salt
1 tbsp olive oil
Sea salt and freshly ground black pepper
2 tomatoes, skinned, seeded and finely chopped
3 tbsp finely chopped fresh coriander

SERVES 6-8

Peel the avocados and scoop their flesh into a large bowl, removing any discoloured bits. Mash with a fork until you have a chunky paste. Pour the lime juice over, then add the finely chopped onion, chilli, crushed garlic and olive oil and mix in well. Season with salt and black pepper to taste, then stir in the chopped tomatoes and fresh coriander.

Cover and refrigerate until ready to serve, but don't make it much more than an hour in advance.

STICKY HONEY & MUSTARD SAUSAGES

I don't care what marvellously clever and sophisticated canapés hit the headlines, this is still everyone's favourite party snack. You must however – as with all sausage recipes – use decent sausages. If you can't find a good mini-chipolata cut an ordinary chipolata in half.

1 tbsp sunflower oil or light olive oil
500g mini chipolata sausages or ordinary chipolatas, halved
2 tbsp clear honey
1 tbsp grain mustard
$\frac{1}{4}$ tsp ground ginger or English mustard powder (optional)
A supply of cocktail sticks

Heat the oven to 190 C/375 F/Gas 5. Pour a little oil into a large baking tin. Cut the links between the sausages, tip them into the tin and turn them in the oil so they're all lightly coated. Roast for about 12-15 minutes until lightly browned, shaking the pan occasionally.

Mix together the honey and mustard, adding a little ginger or English mustard if you think it needs zipping up. (It shouldn't be spicy though – that's the whole point.) Pour off the excess fat that has accumulated from the sausages and pour the honey mixture over. Give the pan a good shake to coat the sausages, then return to the oven for about 10 minutes until the sausages become brown, gooey and sticky, shaking the pan again half way through to flip the sausages over. Transfer the sausages to a plate and leave to cool for 5-6 minutes (see footnote). Serve with cocktail sticks.

Fill your roasting tin with boiling water and leave to soak immediately you've used it, otherwise it will be a pig to clean.

MINI SAUSAGE CROISSANTS

I got the idea of popping party sausages in ready-made croissant dough from watching cookery presenter Silvano Franco on TV last year. It makes a better sausage roll than a bought one (always provided you use a decent sausage) and is much quicker and easier than making them from scratch yourself.

16 small chipolatas
1 tbsp sunflower oil or other cooking oil
2 tubes of Sara Lee or other chilled croissant dough
Some honey-flavoured mustard/grain mustard/ketchup/relish – whatever you fancy flavouring the croissants with
1 medium egg, lightly beaten
2-3 tsp sesame seeds

SERVES 8-10

Brown the chipolatas lightly in the oil on all sides in a frying pan. Unroll the dough and cut through the marked out pieces. Cut each piece of dough into two so that you have 2 even-sized triangles and roll them out slightly bigger with a rolling pin. Put a dab of mustard, ketchup or relish in the centre of each piece of croissant dough and roll it up around a sausage, sticking the edges together with a little of the beaten egg. (These won't be even and tidy but that adds to their charm.)

Heat the oven to 200 C/400 F/Gas 6. Lay the croissants out on one or two lightly greased baking sheets and brush the remaining egg over the tops. Sprinkle over the sesame seeds then bake for about 10-12 minutes, until puffy and nicely browned.

You can prepare these ahead and refrigerate them before baking them if you like.

Do buy proper mini chipolatas from a butcher or sausage specialist rather than those vile pink, pasty mini-sausages.

ALL-YEAR CHRISTMAS DINNER

One of the reasons I suspect we don't eat Christmas dinner other than at Christmas, is that cooking a turkey brings one perilously close to a nervous breakdown. In fact, if it wasn't for the blasted bird we'd probably have it all the time. The other elements – sausages, bacon, stuffing, roast potatoes, sprouts, gravy, bread sauce and cranberry sauce are all perfectly do-able. Or at least any three or four of them are at a time.

Obviously, being a sausage book, sausages are non-negotiable, though I've no objection to sausage meat turning into stuffing (see pp136-137).

Gravy you can find on p34. Roast potatoes, I'm sure you know how to do already. As the whole point of the exercise is minimising effort I suggest you buy the cranberry sauce, but bread sauce is definitely worth making from scratch and here's how to do it.

CIABATTA & GARLIC SAUCE

Unless you've got a good baker, it's better to make bread sauce with a bread that has some substance to it, like ciabatta. Having outraged traditionalists you might as well add the garlic too which actually works very well. You could even use this as a substitute for mash or instead of (shock! horror!) roast potatoes.

1 small onion, peeled and halved
6 cloves
1 large clove of garlic, peeled
1 bay leaf
275ml whole milk
1 ciabatta roll or $1/3$ of a ciabatta or about 75g really good quality white bread
Salt and freshly ground black pepper
Freshly grated nutmeg
10g butter

1 tbsp finely chopped fresh parsley (optional)
Salt and freshly ground black pepper

Stud the onion halves with the cloves, place them in a small non-stick saucepan with the garlic and bay leaf, pour over the milk and bring just to the boil. Set aside to infuse for 20-30 minutes. Cut the crust off the ciabatta without removing too much of the crumb, break it up and whizz it up in a food processor to make fine breadcrumbs. Strain the milk, return it to the pan, add the breadcrumbs and heat gently for 10-15 minutes until thick, stirring frequently to prevent it from sticking. Season with salt, pepper and freshly grated nutmeg. Just before serving, add the butter and finely chopped parsley, if using.

SPROUTS WITH BACON & CHESTNUTS

I am, I'm afraid, afflicted with a missionary zeal about sprouts, which I feel are a much maligned and misunderstood vegetable. Being a member of the cabbage family they also go very well with sausages. Here's how to win over sceptics.

450g fresh sprouts
   (please don't use frozen)
1 tbsp olive oil
110g dry-cure smoked streaky bacon,
   cut into smallish pieces
   (easiest with scissors)
110g cooked chestnuts, halved
A pinch of allspice
Salt and freshly ground black pepper
15g butter

Peel any damaged outer leaves off the sprouts and cut a cross in the base of the larger ones to help them cook evenly. Put them in a saucepan and pour over enough boiling water just to cover. Add salt, bring to the boil and simmer for about 10 minutes until you can stick a knife in them without any resistance.

Meanwhile, heat a frying pan over a moderate heat, add the oil and tip in the bacon. Fry for 3-4 minutes until the bacon fat begins to run, then add the chestnuts and continue to fry until the bacon is crisp (about another 3 minutes). Toss the drained sprouts with the bacon and chestnuts and season with a pinch of allspice, plenty of freshly ground black pepper and a little salt (depending how salty the bacon is). Add the butter, toss again and serve with fried or grilled chipolatas.

SAUSAGE & BACON ROLLS

Could be the centrepiece of your all-year Christmas feast. You may be tempted to sex them up by making them with pancetta rather than bacon but it is quite needlessly extravagant – not to say unpatriotic. Just use a decent dry-cure streaky bacon. The one produced by Denhay Farms (www.denhay.co.uk) is particularly good.

400g chipolatas
200g thinly sliced, smoked dry-cure
   streaky bacon (see above)
1 tbsp oil

Pre-heat the oven to 190 C/375 F/Gas 5. Unlink the sausages. Lay each rasher of bacon flat on a chopping board and run the back of a knife down the rasher to flatten it out and extend it. Wind it round one of the chipolatas and repeat with the rest of the bacon and sausages.

Pour the oil into a roasting tin, swirl it around and lay the sausages in the tin.

Bake them for 20 minutes then turn the heat up to 225 C/425 F/Gas 7 and cook for another 6-7 minutes to crisp up the bacon.

If you're making this to accompany a chicken or turkey, cut the chipolatas and bacon rashers in half so the sausage rolls look smaller and cuter.

142 D.I.Y. SAUSAGES
148 THE SAUSAGE STORECUPBOARD
152 WHERE TO BUY A GOOD SAUSAGE
154 WHAT TO DRINK WITH A SAUSAGE

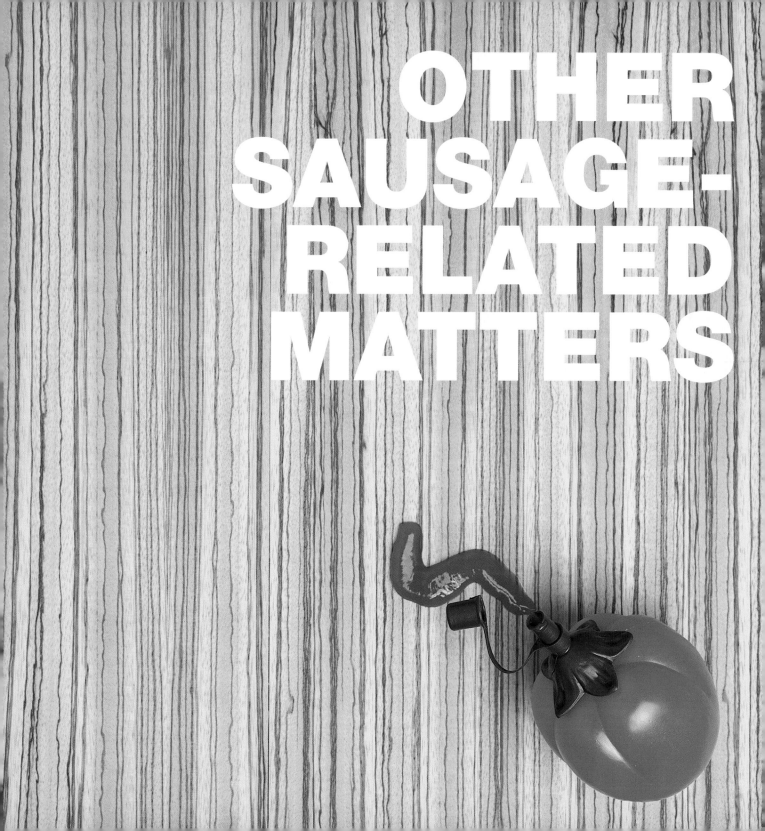

OTHER SAUSAGE-RELATED MATTERS

D.I.Y. SAUSAGES

We agonised long and hard about whether to include information about how to make your own sausages.
When I say we, I don't mean the royal 'we' but me and Meg, my editor. Georgia, our photographer, was in favour but she was ruthlessly overruled, our general feeling being that life was too short to stuff a sausage and that given quality time in the kitchen there are more rewarding ways to fill it than messing around with pig's intestines.

We're not, however, trying to deprive you of the fun of making up your own sausage recipes which you can perfectly well do without stuffing them into skins.

The advantage – apart from giving an outlet to your creativity – is that you know exactly what is going into your sausage, and that you can use fresh herbs, exotic spices and other ingredients that most butchers can't or won't afford.

It may help at this juncture to re-read the pages on what makes a good sausage on p9. Obviously that involves minced meat of some kind. Your butcher may be willing to mince whatever meat you choose for you but may not be able to handle the small quantities you need for an experimental batch. If you have a mincer attachment on your mixer you're laughing. Otherwise look around for a hand-cranked mincer, which you can still find in antique shops and charity shops.

You can also cheat (as I sometimes do) by making part of the mix from skinned, good quality sausages; a trick that saves you having to mess around with breadcrumbs or egg and makes a smooth 'sausage' that won't fall apart. You can form them into any shape you want – small patties, meatballs, Scotch eggs, even a meat loaf. There is, of course, a danger that you'll get so hooked on making your own that you'll find yourself instantly investing in mixers with sausage-making attachments and sending off for consignments of hog casings (see p153), but I can't be held responsible for that....

KOFTE KEBABS WITH FRESH HERBS & GARLIC

These Turkish-inspired sausages, which you wrap round skewers, are great to grill or barbecue.
Or simply form them into flat patties and cook them on a ridged grill or dryish frying pan.

1 small- to medium-sized onion, peeled,
    quartered and roughly chopped
500g minced beef
500g minced lamb
2 large cloves of garlic
1 level tsp ground coriander
1 level tsp ground cumin
$1/2$ level tsp paprika or hot pimenton
2 heaped tbsp each of finely chopped
    coriander and parsley leaves
Leaves of 3-4 sprigs of mint, finely
    chopped
$1/2$ tsp salt
A little oil
A little flour for shaping the kofte

8 metal skewers

SERVES 8

The meat mixture is best made in a food processor, but you may have to do it in two batches. Place the onion in the bowl and pulse until finely chopped but don't over-process. Add the minced beef and lamb, the garlic, ground coriander, cumin, paprika, fresh herbs and salt and process until the seasonings are well amalgamated and the mixture is almost like a paste in texture. Leave for at least half an hour for the flavours to amalgamate.

Divide the meat mixture into 8 portions and lightly oil the skewers. With lightly floured hands, form each into a sausage then insert a skewer into the centre and work the meat around and down it, squeezing it together so that you end up with a long sausage shape.

Place the skewers on a lightly oiled baking tray or foil. Just before cooking, lightly smear the kebabs with oil then grill over pre-heated coals (*see* advice on flare-ups on p126) for about 12-15 minutes until nicely charred. Serve with wedges of lemon, warm pitta bread and a simple tomato, cucumber and onion salad. If making patties for kids serve them like burgers in pitta breads, allowing them to choose toppings such as hummus, raw onion, sliced tomato and cucumber or shredded iceberg lettuce.

ITALIAN-STYLE VEAL, LEMON & PARSLEY SAUSAGES

A good example of the original flavours you can get if you make a sausage mixture from scratch yourself. The flavouring is based on the deliciously punchy Italian seasoning, gremolata.

400g lean stewing veal or pork
(see footnote)
50g pork back fat
50g pancetta or rinded dry-cure streaky
bacon
40g fresh white breadcrumbs
1 rounded tbsp capers, rinsed and
roughly chopped
1-1½ tbsp finely grated lemon zest
1-2 cloves of garlic, peeled and crushed
3 rounded tbsp finely chopped fresh flat
leaf parsley
1 medium egg, lightly beaten
Salt and freshly ground black pepper
Plain flour for shaping
Sunflower or light olive oil for frying

SERVES 3-4

Cut the veal, pork fat and bacon into strips and feed through a mincer. Push a piece of bread through at the end to ensure the last bits of meat come through. Add the breadcrumbs, chopped capers, lemon zest, garlic and parsley to the veal mixture and mix together thoroughly. Add enough of the beaten egg to bind the mixture and season with a little salt and black pepper. Test the mixture for seasoning by frying a small spoonful in a small frying pan, adjusting the seasoning to taste.

Divide the mixture into 8 even-sized portions, each weighing about 70-75g and lay them on a floured board. Flour your hands, then shape each portion into a small rectangle about 7cm long and 3 cm deep, patting it into a sausage shape. Cover them with clingfilm and leave them to chill in the fridge for a couple of hours.

When ready to cook, heat a large frying pan, add a centimetre of oil in the bottom, then fry the sausages lightly on all sides for about 10 minutes, turning them regularly. Serve with Salsa Verde (see p131) and new potatoes, or simply with a wedge of lemon and a watercress, spinach and rocket salad.

You can of course buy your meat ready minced from the butcher, in which case you probably won't need the additional back fat.

Instead of using breadcrumbs and an egg yolk, you could use a couple of skinned, traditional, lightly seasoned sausages to bind the mixture and adjust the seasoning accordingly.

THAI PORK PATTIES WITH CHILLI & CORIANDER DIPPING SAUCE

If you're a lover of Thai fish cakes – and who isn't – here's an equally appealing version for sausage-lovers. I suggest making a large batch, as they'll go amazingly quickly, and you might just as well while you're doing all that chopping. You can also freeze them, provided none of the ingredients has already been frozen.

250g good meaty plain sausages
 or sausage meat
500g minced pork
$^2/_3$ of a bunch of spring onions, trimmed
 and very finely chopped
2 cloves of garlic, peeled and crushed
1$^1/_2$ tsp freshly grated ginger or ginger
 paste
2 small or one large red chilli, de-seeded
 and very finely chopped
Grated rind of 1 lime, preferably unwaxed
6-8 fresh lime leaves or dried lime leaves
 soaked in warm water
2 tbsp finely chopped fresh mint leaves
1$^1/_2$ tbsp fish sauce
Freshly ground white pepper (optional)
A little plain flour for shaping
Oil for frying

For the dipping sauce
2 tbsp lime juice
2 tbsp Japanese rice vinegar
1 tsp light soy sauce or 2 tsp fish sauce
2 small or 1 large red chilli, de-seeded
 and very finely chopped
2 cloves of garlic, peeled and very finely
 chopped
1 tsp freshly grated ginger (optional)
1-2 tsp caster sugar
2 heaped tbsp chopped coriander

MAKES 24 PATTIES

To make the pork patties, slit and slip off the sausage skins. Put the meat in a bowl with the minced pork and mix together well. Add the spring onions, crushed garlic, grated ginger, finely chopped chilli and grated lime zest.

Strip the central rib out of the lime leaves, roll them up and slice them finely, then chop them as small as you can. Add to the pork mixture with the chopped mint, fish sauce and a little white pepper if using. Mix thoroughly (by hand is easiest).

Flour a chopping board. Take a tablespoon of the mixture, dip it in the flour and roll it lightly between your palms, then press down to form a patty. Repeat with the remaining mixture, transferring the finished patties to a baking tray. Refrigerate until ready to cook.

Make the dipping sauce by combining the lime juice, rice vinegar, chopped chilli, garlic and ginger in a bowl. Add 4 tbsp of water and season to taste with caster sugar. Just before serving, stir in the chopped coriander.

Fry the patties in batches in hot oil for about 5 minutes a side or slightly longer if they've been in the fridge. Serve with the dipping sauce.

Alternatively, you could use the dipping sauce as a salad dressing. Serve the patties on crisp little gem lettuce leaves topped with finely shredded carrot and cucumber strips and pour over the dressing.

HENRIETTA GREEN'S GLAMORGAN SAUSAGES

Even though no self-respecting vegetarian would buy this book we had to have a vegetable sausage in here somewhere. Glamorgan sausages are heavenly anyway – an oozy warm cheese and herb rissole that makes a fantastic first course or snack. This is food writer Henrietta Green's version from her website, www.foodloversbritain.com. She says you can make them with any hard cheese that has plenty of flavour, such as Caerphilly, Lancashire or, of course, Cheddar.

140g mature farmhouse Cheddar, grated
170g fresh white breadcrumbs
2 spring onions, finely sliced
3 egg yolks
1¹/₂ tbsp finely chopped parsley
1 tsp mustard powder
Salt and freshly ground black pepper
1 egg white, beaten
Oil for frying

MAKES 12
SMALL SAUSAGES

In a large bowl, mix the cheese with 140g of the breadcrumbs and the spring onions.

In a separate bowl, whisk the egg yolks with the parsley, mustard, salt and pepper, and then mix this into the cheese mixture. You may need an extra egg yolk or a little water if it is too crumbly or dry.

Divide the mixture into 12 equal portions and roll each one into a small sausage about 5cm long. Dip the sausages in egg white and roll them in the remaining breadcrumbs. Heat the oil in a large frying-pan and fry the sausages until golden brown. Drain and serve.

I like to serve these with a tomato chutney or onion marmalade. They're also oddly good with lightly steamed broccoli.

THE SAUSAGE STORECUPBOARD

The two most popular condiments to serve with a sausage give the clue to the qualities you need to set it off to perfection: ketchup and mustard – sweetness and sharpness (or even slight astringency). Obviously the plainer the sausage, the more you need to adorn it. Some of the new, fancy varieties scarcely need anything added by way of flavour.

MUSTARD

Top of my list as a storecupboard staple.
In fact I have several kinds to go with different sausages:

Dijon (I like Maille)
To go with a breakfast sausage or a sausage sarnie.

Whole grain (Tracklements do a good one)
With herby sausages.

Sweet, mild, yellow American mustard (French's)
To go with hot dogs.

There are also some interesting mustard variants. I like Elsenham's Tewkesbury, a mixture of mustard and horseradish, which goes very well with a beef sausage. And honey-flavoured mustard nicely sets off a cold one. The sharp-eyed among you will notice I've left English mustard off the list. Not a big fan I'm afraid. Too hot first thing in the morning. Too coarse later in the day.

KETCHUP AND SAUCES

I'm not a ketchup enthusiast, though everyone else in the family is. Ketchup though is a better option than mustard when there are chips involved.

Tomato Ketchup
Although I'd rather have low-salt and low-sugar versions in the house, it really has to be Heinz (and squeezable).

Brown Sauce
My husband (appropriately enough) goes for Daddies.
I prefer HP.

AND THE REST...

Sausage and chips are also good with mayo (the French Benedicta brand tastes more home-made than Hellman's) as, of course, are cold sausage sandwiches, preferably accompanied by a sweet pickled cucumber or a few cornichons. Garlic mayo is curiously good with spicy sausages.

Then you need at least one chutney or relish to zip up a leftover sausage. Tomato-based relishes are good. Sweetish fruity chutneys like Baxters Victorian are good. Piccallili is very good. I don't like Branston pickle with a sausage, but then I don't much like Branston anyway. Mild Indian-spiced chutneys such as Geeta's can be nice, but not those ferocious lime pickles which override the subtle sweetness of the British sausage.

Onions in any form are great. You can now buy onion marmalade, as they bizarrely insist on calling it (celebrity chefs to blame here, I fear), but it's easy enough to make your own (see p151). Easy too are the appropriately named Eazy Onions, a Spanish product which comes in tins and which is deliciously sweet. They benefit from being zipped up with a little balsamic vinegar, which also has the effect of deepening the colour. They also need to be served hot.

Finally a word on salt. Most sausages are pretty salty anyway so try to lay off it at the table. Except on chips of course.

BRAMLEY APPLE, ONION & CIDER SAUCE

Apple sauce is just as good an accompaniment to sausages as it is to roast pork.
A fresh-tasting, light and zesty alternative to gravy.

2 tbsp light olive oil
10g butter
1 large onion (about 250g), peeled and
   finely sliced
2 large or 3-4 smaller Bramley apples
   (about 650g in total)
100ml dry cider
1 level tsp chopped fresh thyme leaves
   (don't use dried thyme)
1 tbsp finely chopped parsley or chives
Salt, pepper and sugar to taste

SERVES 4-6

Heat the oil and butter in a medium to large saucepan. When the butter has melted, tip in the sliced onions, give them a good stir, put a lid on the pan and let them cook over a low heat for 10 minutes, stirring them occasionally, until they are soft. In the meantime, quarter and peel the Bramley apples. Slice them into the pan, add the cider and thyme, stir, bring to the boil, lower the heat, replace the lid and leave to simmer for 10-15 minutes until the apples have collapsed. (How long this takes depends on the apples.)

Beat the sauce with a wooden spoon to fluff up the apples (you may have to mash more obstinate bits with a fork), then season with salt, pepper and a little sugar, if you think it needs it. Stir in the chopped parsley or chives. Good with a plain or herby pork sausage.

STICKY BARBECUE SAUCE

With so many branded sauces on the market you may wonder why it's worth bothering making your own.
Simple – it tastes better.

500g jar creamed tomatoes or passata
75g dark brown muscovado sugar
75ml (5 tbsp) cider vinegar
1 tbsp Worcestershire sauce
1 tbsp mild chilli powder
A few drops (or more) of hot chilli sauce
2 large cloves of garlic, peeled and
   crushed
1/4 tsp salt

SERVES 6

Combine all the ingredients in a saucepan, bring to the boil then simmer for 10 minutes or until the sauce starts to thicken and plop. Check the seasoning, adding extra chilli sauce if you think it needs it.

You can serve this as a pour-on sauce or brown the sausages lightly first then pour the sauce over, ensuring they are thoroughly coated. Then cook in a moderate oven 190 C/375 F/Gas 5 for about 40 minutes, turning the sausages

regularly until the sauce has all but disappeared and the sausages are lovely and sticky. (Stir in a little boiling water if they seem to be getting too dry.) Serve with baked potatoes and coleslaw.

ONION MARMALADE

I'm afraid to achieve successful Onion Marmalade you have to make it in small batches, as and when you need it – not that it's a remotely difficult thing to do.

3 tbsp olive oil
4 medium red onions, peeled and thinly
  sliced (about 400g)
15g butter
1 tsp balsamic vinegar
Salt and freshly ground black pepper

SERVES 3-4

Heat a large frying pan or wok and add the oil. Fry the onions over a moderately high heat, stirring them occasionally until soft and well browned (about 10 minutes). Add the butter, turn the heat down a little and continue to fry, stirring, for another 5 minutes. Stir in a teaspoon of balsamic vinegar and season to taste with salt and pepper.

RIPE TOMATO CHUTNEY

A simple, very English chutney from one of my all-time favourite food writers Katie Stewart, whose books I consulted regularly when I was learning to cook. I've tweaked it very slightly to take account of today's ingredients.

2.7kg ripe tomatoes
225g onions
300ml distilled white vinegar
1 tbsp salt
A pinch of mixed spice
1 level tsp sweet pimenton
1 rounded tsp hot pimenton
350g unrefined granulated sugar

MAKES 1.8KG
(4 x 450G JARS)

Make a small nick in the skin of the tomatoes near the stalk and drop them, a few at a time, into a saucepan of boiling water. Leave for 30-60 seconds, then lift out with a perforated spoon and place in a bowl of cold water. Peel away the skins, cut up the tomato flesh and place in a large stainless steel saucepan or preserving pan. Chop the onions, place in a small saucepan and just cover with cold water. Bring to the boil, simmer for 5 minutes then drain and add the onions to the tomatoes. Cook the onions and tomatoes over a moderate heat until the liquid has reduced and the mixture is thick. (Ripe tomatoes have a high percentage of water and must be well reduced otherwise there is a danger that the vinegar will be diluted and the finished chutney will not keep well.)

Add half the vinegar, the salt and the spices and simmer for 30 minutes until thick. Dissolve the sugar in the remaining vinegar and add to the mixture. Simmer gently for a further 1-2 hours until all the vinegar has been absorbed and the mixture is quite thick. (A wooden spoon drawn across the mixture should leave a trail.) Pour into clean, dry, warmed jars and cover with plastic-lined jam jar lids. Store the chutney for a couple of months before using to allow the flavours to mellow. Perfect with a warm, rather than hot sausage – plain or herby.

WHERE TO BUY A GOOD SAUSAGE

These days the sausage-lover is spoilt for choice. You can buy a good sausage anywhere – and a bad one, it has to be said. Price, above all, is the key.

SUPERMARKETS

Supermarkets are going to be the first port of call for most of us and their top end ranges (products like Sainsbury's 'Taste the Difference' and Tesco's 'Finest') all tend to be pretty good these days. I'm less impressed with their mid-priced sausages, which include more traditional varieties such as Lincolnshire and can be rather smooth and pasty. A question of taste, I appreciate, although I would always check the label for the meat content. Two good brands stocked by supermarkets are Eastbrook Farm and Duchy Originals.

BUTCHERS

A good butcher's sausage is hard to beat. Generally, the plainer the better. (Butchers don't always handle the more adventurous flavours well.) Two I'd like to single out are:

Eastwoods of Berkhamsted
01442 865012
My local award-winning butcher.

The Ginger Pig
020 7935 7788
Has shops in Marylebone High Street and Borough Market, down by London Bridge. Borough Market is, in fact, a fantastic place to buy sausages. Other good outlets there are Brindisa, Northfield Farm and Sillfield Farm (see opposite).

SPECIALIST SAUSAGE SHOPS

There is a growing number of specialist sausage shops, many of whom now supply by mail order or online.

Simply Sausages in Smithfield
0207 329 3227
One of the first and best.

The Bath Sausage Shop
01225 318300
Highly rated by my publishers who are lucky enough to have it on the doorstep.

Cowmans Famous Sausage Shop Clitheroe
01200 423842
So famous it's now a tourist attraction.

The Masham Sausage Shop
01765 650200
www.mashamsausages.co.uk
Another mecca for Northern sausage lovers.

Crombie's of Edinburgh
0131 5570111
www.sausages.co.uk
Sells over 50 varieties.

PRODUCERS

You can also, of course, order sausages direct from the farm. There are so many good producers now that it seems invidious to single any out, except for those ones of which I have positive first-hand experience:

Graig Farm Organics in Wales
01597 851655
www.graigfarm.co.uk

Northfield Farm
01664 474271
www.northfieldfarm.com
Rare breeds specialist.

Sillfield Farm of Kendal in Cumbria
015395 67609
www.sillfield.co.uk
Specialises in wild boar.

Swaddles Green Organic Farm, Chard
0845 456 1768
www.swaddles.co.uk

The Essex Pig Company

www.essexpigcompany.com.
Jimmy's Doherty's farm shop. You can order from him on-line.

OTHER SAUSAGE SPECIALISTS

There are also suppliers who specialise in particular types of sausage.

Richard Woodall of Cumbria

01229 71723
www.richardwoodall.co.uk
Great for those with a weakness for Cumberland sausages. Has a royal warrant from the Queen.

Clonakilty black (and white) puddings

www.clonakiltyblackpudding.ie
The best come from this producer in West Cork. Stocked here by specialist butchers and department stores.

I Camisa, Old Compton Street, Soho

0207 437 7610
My favourite Italian sausages (possibly even my all-time favourite sausages) come from this Italian deli.

Brindisa, Exmouth Market and Borough Market, London

020 7713 1666
www.brindisa.com

Where to buy authentic Spanish chorizo and morcilla (black pudding). Their products are also stocked by Selfridges.

For more leads on good sausages log onto the excellent www.sausagelinks.co.uk which gives weblinks for many good producers. Henrietta Green's encyclopaedic www.foodloversbritain.com and *Rick Stein's Guide to the Food Heroes of Britain* (BBC Books £12.99) will also give you a good steer.

If you're minded to make your own sausages (don't say I didn't warn you!) www. sausagelinks.co.uk again has a good basic guide and links to other useful sites such as www.sausagemaking.org. For hog casings, saltpetre and other sausage making accoutrements, Hugh Fearnley-Whittingstall recommends the Natural Casing Company in Farnham, Surrey (01252 850454).

Finally for those few (surely?) occasions when you can't be bothered to cook a sausage and simply want to go out and eat them the S&M Cafés are the real McCoy. They have four sausage cafés in London including a proper old-fashioned tiled caff in Essex Road, Islington (020 7359 5361). Other notable sausage-related restaurants include the Clifton Sausage Bar in Bristol (01865 761106) and the Sussex Brewery at Emsworth in Hampshire (01243 371533).

If you have any sausages or sausage making establishments you'd like to recommend, e-mail me at **fiona@sausageandmash.co.uk** and I'll spread the word.

WHAT TO DRINK WITH A SAUSAGE

This page is mainly an excuse to extol the virtues of beer with sausages, a combination that had passed me by until I visited a German beer garden for the first time a couple of years ago. There I had a plate of sausage and potato salad washed down with a glass of the sweet local beer, and I have to admit the combination was utterly sublime. I say this not as a regular beer drinker. Those of you who are will not need convincing. But there is a general idea that beer is just for swilling down in quantity and is of no interest with food. Well, when it comes to sausages that couldn't be more wrong. Good beer – and we in Britain have plenty of them too – is the perfect partner for any kind of German or traditional English sausage. Good quality lagers (German or Czech for preference) are great with sausage salads or hot dogs, and a traditional British bottle-conditioned ale is just made for sausage and mash. Beer also makes great gravy (see the Best Ever Sausages with Rich Guinness Gravy recipe on p38).

Not that I'm overlooking cider, which is also fantastic with milder, sweeter sausages, like pork and leek or pork and apple, or in a sausage pie (see pp78-83).

It's only when you come to spicier, Mediterranean sausages with garlic, fennel or chilli that you begin to yearn for a glass of wine. And that should be rich, red and rustic. Wines from southern France, Spain and Italy are perfect. A Faugères. A Minervois. A good Côtes du Rhone Villages. A rioja crianza (more powerful than an older reserva). A lusty Puglian or Sicilian red. If the sausage is spicy or you're having a barbecue, a chunky Australian shiraz or Argentinian malbec. Nothing too grand.

White wine can also be very enjoyable with the kind of dishes you'd expect it to go with in other non-sausage related contexts. A dry Italian white with a sausage risotto for example. A sauvignon blanc with Thai Sausages with Leek and Lemongrass Rice (see p94). A dry Alsace riesling is excellent with the same sort of dishes that work with lager – like a choucroute. I'm not mad about chardonnay with sausages (except Chablis) but don't let me stop you. White wines go less well than red when there's gravy involved.

Obviously, none of the above applies to breakfast, when a bit more decorum is in order (unless you eat it after 12 noon). A full fry-up definitely calls for a good old-fashioned cup of tea, which for some reason I find goes much better with sausages than coffee. Not Earl Grey. Not a herbal infusion. But proper breakfast tea.

INDEX

A

All-in-one sausage roast *50*
Authentic rough-crushed guacamole *128*

B

Baked sweet potatoes with chilli, lime &
    garlic butter *53*
Barbecue ideas *126-128*

Beef sausage
Sausage, bacon & onion casserole *40*
Sausage chilli *98*
Rigatini with wild boar sausage, red wine
    & rosemary sauce *69*

Best ever sausages with rich Guinness
    gravy *38*
Black pudding with potato, apple & onion
    pan-fry *46*
Braised broad beans with pancetta &
    mint *97*
Bramley apple, onion & cider sauce *150*
Brindisa's hot chorizo & rocket rolls *120*
Broad beans with pancetta & mint,
    Braised *97*
Bubble & squeak *28*

C

cabbage pie, Stuffed *60*
cabbage with red wine & apples, Spiced
    red *63*
Cashel blue & bacon potato cakes *112*
Cassoulet *100*
casserole, Sausage, bacon & onion *40*
cauliflower purée, Heston's amazing *33*
Celeriac & potato mash *26*
Chargrilled potato & chorizo salad *127*

Chilli for chilli dogs *118*
chilli, Sausage *98*
Chinese-style sausages with stir-fried
    greens *58*

Chipolata sausages
Chinese-style sausages with stir-fried
    greens *58*
Mini sausage croissants *134*
Sausage & bacon rolls *139*
Sausage, egg & bacon baps *113*
Sausage, egg & bacon panini *113*
Sticky honey & mustard sausages *132*

chips, with Maldon sea salt, Handcut *42*
Chorizo & butter bean stew *96*
Chorizo, Morcilla & pepper kebabs *128*
chorizo & rocket rolls, Brindisa's hot *120*
chutney, Ripe tomato *151*
Ciabatta & garlic sauce *138*
Classic toad *85*
Colcannon *26*
Colcannon with leeks *28*
Cos lettuce & chive salad *50*
couscous salad & harissa dressing,
    Merguez with warm *106*
Creamy onion, thyme & bay sauce *37*
croissants, Mini sausage *134*
Crushed potatoes with spring onions *29*
Cuban-style avocado, pepper & citrus
    salsa *130*

Cumberland sausages
A good old-fashioned sausage, chicken
    & bacon pie *82*
Best ever sausages with rich Guinness
    gravy *38*
Gordon Ramsey's Cumberland sausage
    boulangère *49*
Modern mixed grill *114*
Pan-fried sausage, apple & prune
    stuffing *137*

D

Devilled kidneys *114*

E

Easy tomato sauce *76*
eggs, Very good Scotch – or maybe
    Welsh – *122*

F

Frankfurters with creamy lentils,
    Grilled *104*
French bistro salad *56*
French style haricots with garlic *96*

G

Garlic & olive oil mash *25*
Glamorgan sausages, Henrietta Green's
    147
Good, everyday mash *24*
good old-fashioned sausage, chicken &
    bacon
    pie, A *82*
good, simple onion gravy, A *34*
Gordon Ramsay's Cumberland sausage
    boulangère *49*
gratin, Sue Lawrence's potato &
    juniper *52*

Gravies
good, simple onion gravy, A *34*
Guinness gravy, Best ever sausages with
    rich *38*
light child-friendly gravy without
    onions, A *36*
onion gravy, A good, simple *34*
Spiced redcurrant & port gravy *36*

Grilled frankfurters with creamy lentils 104
Grilled Luganega sausages with cherry tomato & basil pasta 68
Grilled polenta wedges 73
guacamole, Authentic rough-crushed 128

H

Handcut chips with maldon sea salt 42

Herb Sausages
Classic toad 85
Spicy toad 85
Mini sausage toads 86
Nigel Slater's sausage & potato pie 81

Heston's amazing cauliflower purée 33

Home-made sausages
Henrietta Green's Glamorgan sausages 147
Italian – style veal, lemon & parsley sausages 144
Kofte kebabs with fresh herbs & garlic 143
Thai pork patties with chilli & coriander dipping sauce 146

Hot dogs
The bun 116
The classic 118
Chilli for chilli dogs 118
The hot dog stall special 118
The hot chilli dog 118
The sausage 116
The Wisconsin brat 118

I

Italian sausages
Grilled Luganega sausages with cherry tomato & basil pasta 68
Italian sausage, Mozzarella & artichoke pizza 74
Italian sausage, tomato & basil risotto 90
Quick garlic & fennel sausage pizza 76

Sausage & pepper panini 119
Sausages in red wine with sloppy polenta 72
Savoy cabbage & Luganega sausage soup 62
Vincent Schiavelli's sosizza chi patati (sausage with potatoes) 48

J

jambalaya, Rick Stein's spicy sausage & prawn 92
Jersey potato & broad bean salad with parsley, chives & mint 57

K

kebabs, Chorizo, morcilla & pepper 128
kebabs, with fresh herbs & garlic, Kofte 143
kidneys, Devilled 114

L

Lamb sausages
All-in-one sausage roast 50
Turkish-style lamb sausage, herb & Feta pizza 75

Leek & pea purée 32
lentils, Grilled frankfurters with creamy 104
lentils, Toulouse sausages with puy 102
light, child-friendly gravy without onions, A 36
Luganega sausage soup, Savoy cabbage & 62
Luganega sausages with cherry tomato & basil pasta, Grilled 68
Luxury mash 25

M

Mash
mash, Cerleriac & potato 26
mash, Garlic & olive oil 25
mash, Good everyday 24
mash, Luxury 25
mash, Parmesan & chive 25

meatballs, Spaghetti with 66
Merguez with warm couscous salad & harissa dressing 106
Mini sausage croissants 134
Mini sausage toads 86
Modern mixed grill 114

N

Nigel Slater's sausage & potato pie 81

O

Onion marmalade 151
onion, thyme & bay sauce, Creamy 37

P

Pan-fried sausage, apple & prune stuffing 137
panini, Sausage, egg & bacon 113
panini, Sausage & pepper 119
Parmesan & chive mash 25
Parsnip & nutmeg purée 32
pasta, Grilled Luganega sausages with cherry tomato & basil 68
pasta with capers, olives & Feta, Sicilian sausage 70
pasties, Sausage, potato & dill 124
Patatas bravas 44
Patatas pobres 45
Pico de gallo 130
pie, A good old-fashioned sausage, chicken & bacon 82

pie, Italian-style sausage, spinach & Ricotta 80
pie, Nigel Slater's sausage & potato 81
pie, Sausage, onion & apple 78
pie, Stuffed cabbage 60
pizza, Italian sausage, Mozzarella & artichoke 74
pizza, Quick garlic & fennel sausage 76
pizza, Turkish-style lamb sausage, herb & Feta 75
polenta wedges, Grilled 73
polenta, Sloppy 73

Pork sausages (see also Toulouse & Cumberland listings)
All-in-one sausage roast 50
Classic toad 85
Italian-style sausage, spinach & Ricotta pie 80
Mini sausage toads 86
pork patties with chilli & coriander dipping sauce, Thai 146
Sausage, onion & apple pie 78
Sausage, potato & dill pasties 124
Sausages with white wine 37
Spaghetti with meatballs 66
Spicy chilli 98
Spicy toad 85
Stuffed cabbage pie 60
stuffing, Sausage, chestnut & mushroom 136
Very good Scotch – or maybe Welsh – eggs 122

potato cakes, Cashel blue & bacon 112

Potatoes
Baked sweet potatoes with chilli, lime & garlic butter 53
Bubble & squeak 28
Celeriac & potato mash 26
Colcannon 26
Colcannon with leeks 28
Crushed potatoes with spring onions 29
Garlic & olive oil mash 25
Good, everyday mash 24
Handcut chips with Maldon sea salt 42

Jersey potato & broad bean salad with parsley, chives & mint 57
Luxury mash 25
Parmesan & chive mash 25
Patatas bravas 44
Patatas pobres 45
Roast sweet potatoes with spiced chilli salt 53
Sue Lawrence's potato & juniper gratin 52
Stovies 45

Q

quiche, Sausage, potato & spring onion 125
Quick garlic & fennel sausage pizza 76

R

redcurrant & port gravy, Spiced 36
rice, Spicy sausage & egg-fried 93
rice, Thai sausages with leek & lemongrass 94
Rick Steins's spicy sausage & prawn jambalaya 92
Rigatoni with wild boar sausage, red wine & rosemary sauce 69
Ripe tomato chutney 151
risotto, Italian sausage, tomato & basil 90
Roast sweet potatoes with spiced chilli salt 53

S

salad, Chargrilled potato & chorizo 127
salad, Cos lettuce & chive 50
salad with parsley, chives & mint, Jersey potato & broad bean 57
salad, French bistro 56
Salsa verde 131

Salsas
Cuban-style avocado, pepper & citrus salsa 130

Picp de gallo 130
Salsa verde 131

sauce, Bramley apple, onion & cider 150
sauce, Ciabatta & garlic 138
sauce, Creamy onion, thyme & bay 37
sauce, Easy tomato 76
sauce, Sticky barbecue 150
sauce, Thai pork patties with chilli & coriander dipping 146
Sausage & bacon rolls 139
Sausage, bacon & onion casserole 40
Sausage, chestnut & mushroom stuffing 136
Sausage chilli 98
Sausage, egg & bacon baps 113
Sausage, egg & bacon panini 113
Sausage, egg & cress bap 121
Sausage, onion & apple pie 78
Sausage & pepper panini 119
sausage & potato pie, Nigel Slater's 81
Sausage, potato & dill pasties 124
Sausage, potato & spring onion quiche 125
sausage roast, All-in-one 50
sausage soup, Savoy cabbage & Luganega 62
(sausage with potatoes), Vincent Schiavelli's sosizza chi patati, 48
Sausages in red wine with sloppy polenta 72
sausages, Sticky honey & mustard 132
sausages with rich guinness gravy, Best ever 38
sausages with stir-fried greens, Chinese-style 58
Sausages with white wine 37
Savoy cabbage & Luganega sausage soup 62
SBLTs 121
Schnecke's choucroute 61
Scotch – or maybe Welsh – eggs, Very good 122
Sicilian sausage pasta with capers, olives & Feta 70
Silky swede & carrot purée 30

Sloppy polenta *73*
soup, Savoy cabbage & Luganega
    sausage *62*
Spaghetti with meatballs *66*
Spiced red cabbage with red wine &
    apples *63*
Spiced redcurrant & port gravy *36*

Spicy sausage
Braised broad beans with pancetta &
    mint *97*
Chorizo & butter bean stew *96*
Chorizo, Morcilla & pepper kebabs *128*
chorizo & rocket rolls, Brindisa'a Hot *120*
chorizo salad, Chargrilled potato & *127*
Merguez with warm couscous salad &
    Harissa dressing *106*
Rick Stein's spicy sausage & prawn
    jambalaya *92*
Sausage chilli *98*
Sicilian sausage pasta with capers,
    olives & Feta *70*
Spicy sausage & egg-fried rice *93*
Tarka dal with crispy onions *105*
Thai sausages with leek & lemongrass
    rice *94*

Spicy toad *85*
Sprouts with bacon & chestnuts *139*
stew, Chorizo & butter bean *96*
stew, White sausage & white beer *41*
Sticky barbecue sauce *150*
Sticky honey & mustard sausages *132*
Stovies *45*
Stufffed cabbage pie *60*
stuffing, Pan-fried sausage, apple &
    prune *137*
stuffing, Sausage, chestnut &
    mushroom *136*
Sue Lawrence's potato & juniper gratin *52*
Summer carrot & coriander purée *30*
sweet potatoes with chilli, lime & garlic
    butter, Baked *53*
sweet potatoes with spiced chilli salt,
    Roast *53*

T

Tarka dal with crispy onions *105*
Thai sausages with leek & lemongrass
    rice *94*

Toad in the hole
Classic toad *85*
Spicy toad *85*
Mini sausage toads *86*

tomato sauce, Easy *76*

Toulouse sausage
Cassoulet *100*
Quick garlic & fennel sausage pizza *76*
Sausages in red wine with sloppy
    polenta *72*
Toulouse sausages with puy lentils *102*

Turkish-style lamb sausage, herb & Feta
    pizza *75*

V

veal, lemon & parsley sausages,
    Italian-style *144*

Vegetable purées
Heston's amazing cauliflower purée *33*
Leek & pea purée *32*
Parsnip & nutmeg purée *32*
Silky swede & carrot purée *30*
Summer carrot & coriander purée *30*

Venison sausages
Rigatoni with wild boar sausage, red
    wine & rosemary sauce *69*

Very good Scotch – or maybe Welsh –
    eggs *122*
Vincent Schiavelli's sosizza chi patati
    (sausage with potatoes) *48*

W

White pudding with new potatoes,
    asparagus & peas *54*
White sausage & white beer stew *41*
wild boar sausage, red wine & rosemary
    sauce, Rigatoni with *69*

ACKNOWLEDGMENTS

If evidence were needed of exactly how popular sausages are I have to tell you the family survived almost two months of sausages for dinner without a single complaint. So, first and foremost, a big thank you to them. Thanks too to Paul Hughes and Tim Wilson of The Ginger Pig and Joe Collier and Adam Cullinane of my local butchers, Eastwoods of Berkhamsted, who showed me what goes into a good sausage. The biggest tributes though should go to Meg Avent at Absolute Press, whose brilliant idea the book was and who actually made it happen, to Georgia Glynn Smith, for her fantastic photographs, and to the very talented design team: designer (and fellow Liverpool fan) Matt Inwood, stylist Liz Belton and home economist David Morgan. Who would have thought sausages could look so sexy? (Don't answer that.) Thanks to my publisher Jon Croft for allowing me free rein once again and to Leigh Goodman who has tirelessly promoted the end result. Finally, this book is, above all, for my much-loved son William who has remained curiously resistant to sausage and mash ever since he was small. If this book doesn't bring you round, Will, I give up.

ABOUT THE AUTHOR

Fiona Beckett is an ardent sausage-lover and award-winning journalist who has written for most of the national press, from the People to the Guardian. She currently writes on food and drink for the Financial Times, Sainsbury's Magazine and is contributing editor to the wine magazine Decanter. She's written nine other books, including two student cookbooks, *Beyond Baked Beans* and *Beyond Baked Beans Green*, and runs their accompanying website www.beyondbakedbeans.com. All of which leaves not nearly enough time to spend with her long-suffering friends and family or following the fortunes of Liverpool Football Club.

CONVERSION TABLE

Do keep to either metric or imperial measures throughout the whole recipe. Mixing the two can lead to all kinds of problems.

25g	**1 oz**	275g	**10 oz**	5ml	**1 tsp**
50g	**2 oz**	300g	**11 oz**	15ml	**1 tbsp**
75g	**3 oz**	350g	**12 oz**	150ml	**1/4 pint**
100g	**4 oz**	375g	**13 oz**	300ml	**1/2 pint**
150g	**5 oz**	400g	**14 oz**	450ml	**3/4 pint**
175g	**6 oz**	425g	**15 oz**	600ml	**1 pint**
200g	**7 oz**	450g	**16 oz (1lb)**	1.2l	**2 pints**
225g	**8 oz**	1kg	**2 lb**		
250g	**9 oz**				

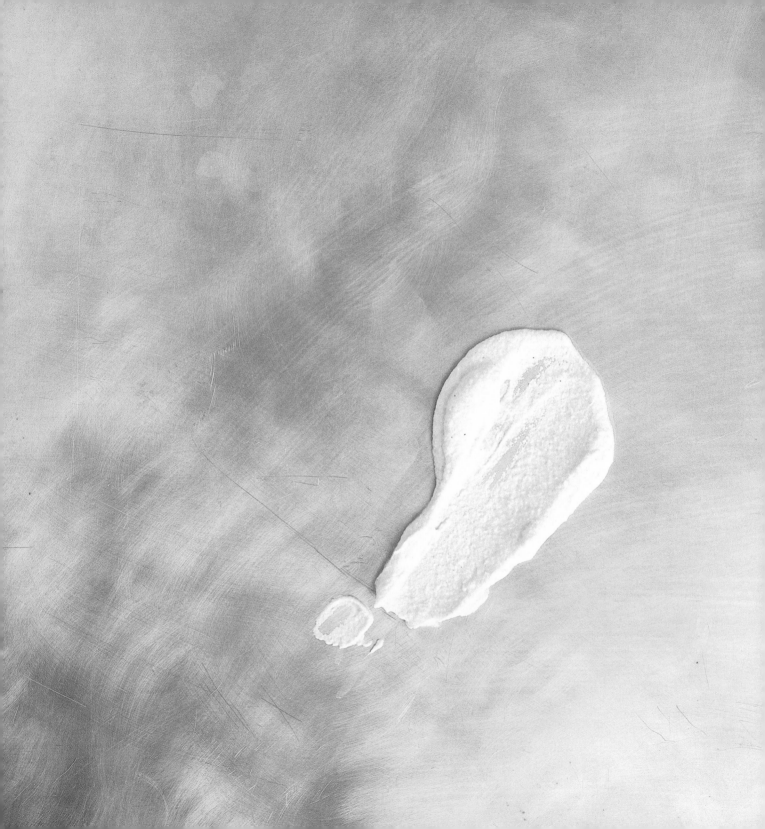